# CHESTER

Text by
MARIAN SUGDEN

Photographs by
ERNEST FRANKL

## PEVENSEY
### Heritage Guides

# Chester

The Victorians created a glorious Tudor fantasy of patterned timber, gables and posts on the storeys above Chester's famous 13th-century Rows. The Rows are covered galleries above the shops at street level, and form second streets where people can stroll beside yet more shops. The visitor can also walk the city walls, which form the most complete circuit of any town in England.

## PLACES TO SEE

### A Eastgate
The simple 18th-century archway forms an airy walkway, which emerges from between the upper storeys of the houses on Eastgate Street.

### B King Charles's Tower
The tower houses an exhibition recounting Chester's role in the Civil War, from the Parliamentary siege of the city in 1643 to the defeat of the Royalist stronghold three years later.
*Apr-Oct, Sat and Sun 11am-5pm. Adm charge. Tel (0244) 321616/318780.*

### C Water Tower

### D Watergate Street
Some of the city's finest timbered buildings line Watergate Street.

### E Town Hall
The giant Victorian Gothic building is composed of bands of red and grey sandstone, and is surmounted by a tower 160ft high. In the Waiting Hall, beneath friezes of the city's history, hangs the Chester Tapestry, woven in 1975 from brightly coloured Wilton carpet wool and depicting the River Dee meandering beside the city's landmarks.
*All year, Mon-Fri. Free entry. Tel (0244) 324324.*

### F Chester Cathedral
Modest nobility rather than grandeur is the impression given by the elegant tower of Chester Cathedral, and by the decorated stonework of the building's reddish walls, parapets and turrets.

### G Heritage Centre
*All year, Mon-Sat 11am-5pm, Sun 12-5pm. Tel (0244) 317948.*

### H Grosvenor Museum
*All year, Mon-Sat and pm Sun. Free entry. Tel (0244) 321616.*

### I Chester Castle
*English Heritage. All year, daily 10am-4pm. Free entry. Cheshire Military Museum: All year, daily. (Closed for Christmas for 2 weeks). Adm charge. Tel (0244) 327617.*

### J St John's Church

### K Amphitheatre
Built in around AD 86, it could hold some 7000 spectators, making it the largest stone amphitheatre discovered in Britain when it was excavated in 1929.

A56
Ellesmere Port 8
Warrington 20

Railway station ¼

**B**

**F**

**E**
ℹ️

FRODSHAM STREET

**P**

**P**

**P**

♿

ST WERBURGH ST

**A**

WC

FOREGATE ST

NORTHGATE ST

EASTGATE ST

ST JOHN STREET

**P**

LITTLE ST JOHN ST

**J**

**K**

BRIDGE STREET

**G** WC

PEPPER STREET

SOUTER'S LANE

♿

GROSVENOR STREET

LOWER BRIDGE STREET

River trips

Suspension Bridge

**H**

CASTLE STREET

**I**

Old Dee Bridge

GROSVENOR ROAD

River Dee

**P**

A Pevensey Heritage Guide

First published 1986
Revised Edition 1993

Photographs: Ernest Frankl, except 30: Tom Ward, the Grosvenor Museum; 56: English Heritage; 73: Lady Lever Gallery, Port Sunlight; 1, 51, 52, 53 are reproduced by kind permission of the Dean and Chapter of the Cathedral

Colour map copyright © The Reader's Digest Association Ltd
All other maps by Carmen Frankl

A catalogue record for this book is available from the British Library.

ISBN 0 907115 65 9

Design by Book Production Consultants, Cambridge
Printed in Hong Kong by Wing King Tong Co. Ltd
for David & Charles plc
Brunel House  Newton Abbot  Devon

The Pevensey Press is an imprint of David & Charles plc

*Front cover*
Half-timbered shops on the corner of Eastgate Street and Bridge Street

*Back cover*
Little Moreton Hall; The Cathedral at dusk; a 'cottage orné' in Marford

*Title page inset*
The Old Dee Bridge and the Bridgegate, from the south of the river. There has been a bridge here since Roman times – many wooden constructions were wrecked by flooding; this one in stone dates from the late 14th century. It was widened in 1826, but much of the original structure remains. A toll was levied on vehicles and animals crossing the bridge until the beginning of 1885

# Contents

# Historic Chester

## Introduction

The history of Chester spans two thousand years, and for centuries it has been a popular centre for travellers and tourists. Daniel Defoe thought Chester 'a city well worth describing', and he does so in his *Tour Through the Whole Island of Great Britain* (1724): 'The best ornament of the city, is, that the streets are very broad and fair . . . The walls, as I have said, are in very good repair, and it is a very pleasant walk around the city, upon the walls, and within the ·battlements, from whence you may see the county around'. Handel stayed here in 1742, forced by bad weather to delay his journey to Dublin for the première of the *Messiah,* and took advantage of the time to rehearse the choruses with local people in the cathedral. Henry James arrived here from America in the 1870s, and in the opening chapters of *The Ambassadors* (1903) describes the curious enchantment of his first taste of the Old World. He gets an agreeable shiver from 'the wicked old Rows of Chester, rank with feudalism', and takes moonlit walks on the walls, 'pausing here and there for a dismantled gate or a bridged gap, with rises and drops, steps up and steps down, queer twists, queer contacts, peeps into homely streets and under the brows of gables, views of cathedral tower and waterside fields, of huddled English town and ordered English country'.

A walk on the walls is not so very different today, and such change as there has been in the last hundred years is largely in the interests of conservation and successful traffic management. The Roman and medieval foundations of the city can still be clearly made out (and are described in the walks outlined in this book), and an extensive programme of archaeological study continues, but Chester is far from being a place of purely antiquarian interest: it is an excellent shopping centre; the races on the Roodee are a high point of the flat-racing year; there are regattas on the river, and a summer festival of music and drama; and the zoo (see pp. 78–80) is world famous.

The characteristic and immediately striking black and white buildings belong as much to the Victorian period as to the Middle Ages – it can be an amusing exercise for the visitor to try to distinguish the one from the other. For anyone wishing to comprehend in detail the evolution and variety of the domestic architecture of the city, the Heritage Centre at St Michael's in Bridge Street has a wealth of attractively displayed information and explanation (see p. 71).

Although motor traffic is partially restricted in the centre of the city, the inner ring road (shown on the map on the inside front cover) follows a course immediately outside the walls and so gives easy access to generous parking facilities in Frodsham Street and Upper Northgate Street, below the castle

**2** *The Abbey Gateway leads from the cathedral precinct of Abbey Square into Northgate Street. This powerful vaulted archway was built in the 14th century, the middle period of building activity in and around the cathedral. The upper storey of the archway was rebuilt in the late 18th or early 19th century. Looming above the gateway is the 160-foot central tower of the town hall.*

near the riverside and Grosvenor Bridge, and in the Grosvenor Precinct off Pepper Street (from which it is a short walk to the Visitor Centre in Vicar's Lane, or to the tourist information centre in Northgate Street).

The disabled visitor can enjoy the entire city centre from the streets, and a short section of the walls may be reached via ramps at Abbey Street and Mercia Square. Bridge Street Row may be reached via the Grosvenor Precinct from its Eastgate entrance next to the Grosvenor Hotel. The tourist information centre sells a specialised guide to shops, restaurants, and public buildings, entitled *Chester for the Disabled*.

The surrounding counties of Cheshire, Clwyd and Merseyside have much to offer the tourist. A Leisure Drive is clearly signposted from Chester, and affords a round trip of some fifty miles, or short excursions of a few miles at a time. It takes in a number of attractive villages, craft centres, gardens, a working mill and a motor museum, besides indicating walks and picnic sites. A small selection from among many possible delights is suggested in the last section of this book.

## Roman Chester

The Romans established Chester, or Deva, as they called it (after the River

*3 The red sandstone of the Peckforton Hills, seen in this Cheshire landscape near Beeston, was used in the construction of many buildings in Chester, including the cathedral and Grosvenor Bridge.*

*4 The wood frame of Mappin and Webb's shop in Eastgate Street Row is structural rather than decorative, unlike some of the 19th-century imitations. The black and white simplicity contrasts starkly with the High Victorian Gothic of Brown's Crypt Building next door. Inside is an intricately carved mantelpiece depicting the port of Chester and the Old Dee Bridge.*

Dee), as a military camp in the middle of the first century AD. Their mighty army, forty to fifty thousand strong, under the Emperor Claudius, had invaded Britain in AD 43, and had subjected first the southern half of the country and then the Welsh, before pushing on northwards to conquer the Scots. Chester provided a strategic position from which they could control their communications to the north, and defend themselves against the Welsh on the one hand, and the unruly Brigantes of the Pennines on the other, and later also against the marauding Irish. The River Dee was tidal as far as Chester, the first point at which it could be easily crossed, and open to the sea (traces of the Roman harbour wall have been found near the modern Roodee racecourse, below Black Friars).

In addition to its strategic importance, its navigable river and its road to London (the *via devana*), Chester had considerable commercial significance for the Romans: copper was mined in Anglesey (annexed in the third century), gold, coal and lead in North Wales, and salt in Cheshire (see p. 88). The surrounding plain was fertile, building material was easily quarried, and the climate was equable, as it still is, seldom reaching extremes of heat or cold. It may not be too fanciful to suggest that the Roman eye for an attractive location was caught by the similarity between the Apennines and the low Welsh hills and peaks to the west of Chester.

The original fortification was of wood, as was the river bridge. The first stone walls were built about AD 100, and extensively reconstructed some two

**5** *Ye Olde Edgar, on the corner of Shipgate Street and Lower Bridge Street, is a 17th-century house, and is said to be slightly older than the nearby Bear and Billet (**40**). In 1845 it was converted from an inn into two private houses. The name commemorates the Mercian King Edgar, who visited Chester in 973, when he was rowed on the river by nine Celtic kings who were subject to him.*

**6** *Ruins of the Norman lady chapel and the 14th-century choir chapels at the east end of St John's church: these parts fell into disuse when the church lost its collegiate status at the time of the Dissolution of the monasteries (see also* **59***).*

and three centuries later (the quarry face can still be seen in Edgar's Field, see p. 76); parts of them are visible to the east of the Northgate (see Walk 2). During more peaceful periods the city was a garrison rather than a centre of active campaigning, and already by the end of the first century it was being settled as a 'citizen fortress', like York and Caerleon, where discharged legionary soldiers would take up permanent residence. The town was laid out on a rectangular plan, with the four main streets running east–west (the *via principalis*, now Eastgate Street and Watergate Street), and north–south (the *via decumana*, now Northgate Street, and the *via praetoria*, now Bridge Street). The headquarters of the military government (the *principia*) were situated centrally, at the crossing of these main streets, in the sector where we now see St Peter's church, the market and the town hall. The deepest foundations of many of today's shops are Roman; excavations for the Grosvenor Precinct in the early 1960s revealed a gymnasium, a bath house and barrack buildings. The amphitheatre, outside the walls to the south-east, is said to be the largest Roman monument in Britain; it would have been capable of accommodating as many as eight thousand people, and was used mainly for military exercise, and less frequently for executions, and for entertainments such as gladiator and beast shows. It has been opened up in recent years, though not completely, for much remains buried beneath modern buildings.

Rebuilding and alteration to the city's road system have afforded welcome opportunities to archaeologists, although their work has often been hard pressed by the developers' timetables. Excavations have been made further afield too: Heronbridge, to the south, is the site of a Roman dock where coal was unloaded, and further south at Holt there was a tile factory, whose products were transported by river. The Grosvenor Museum (see p. 36) houses in its Roman Stones Gallery an important collection of artefacts, monuments, gravestones and memorials from the various excavations, besides a wealth of information about the military organisation and domestic life of the Roman city.

## From Medieval to Tudor

Little is known of Chester's history in the period following the Roman withdrawal from Britain in the 5th century, and the power struggles of the Anglo-Saxon kings and princelings have left no trace. However, it is clear that the cathedral lies on the site of an Anglo-Saxon church, dedicated to St Werburgh and founded in the early 10th century. In 1092 Hugh I, Earl of Chester (see below), asked Anselm, Abbot of Bec, and later Archbishop of Canterbury, to reorganise the church as a Benedictine monastery. The abbey was dissolved in 1540 but was made the cathedral of the diocese by Henry VIII in the following year, when the last abbot became the first dean. The church of St John (see p. 76) is known to have been founded in the late 6th or

**7** *The Mersey Estuary at sunset, with the light catching the silt that has had such a profound effect on Chester's history.*

**8** *The Water Tower, built in 1322, provided a powerful fortification for Chester's harbour. At that time the River Dee flowed close to the walls, but was already silting up. The water to the right of the tower is the Dee Basin.*

early 7th century, with stone taken from the nearby Roman amphitheatre. For a time at the end of the 11th century this church was the cathedral of the diocese of Lichfield and Coventry, and it retained this status even after the removal of the see to Coventry in 1102. Although it is incomplete, it is the most significant Norman building in the area.

According to local legend, after the Norman invasion of 1066 King Harold was not killed in battle at Hastings but fled to Chester and ended his life there as a hermit in a cell near the river (see p. 76). Certainly William the Conqueror lost no time in marching north, across the Pennines, to subdue the

13

rebellious native population. The building of the castle, which was to become a powerful fortress, was begun (probably on the site of a previous Saxon fortification), and the hereditary earldom of Chester was created, first for Gherbod, a Fleming, and later in favour of William's nephew, Hugh d'Avranches. The title reverted to the crown in 1237, however, when Earl John died without an heir. Hugh d'Avranches was known as Hugh Lupus, 'the Wolf' – perhaps on account of his reputedly ruthless and rapacious character and his savage conquest of North Wales, or because he had chosen the wolf emblem for his coat of arms and standards. The name reappeared when the 19th-century Grosvenors, dukes of Westminster, adopted this ancient nickname as their surname.

Cheshire became a county palatine, as did both Durham and Lancashire, virtually a kingdom within a kingdom, entitled to administer justice and raise taxes independently of central government – there had already been a mint here before the Normans arrived. It is still officially called County Palatine, although the term has no modern significance. Edward I created his son, Edward of Caernarfon, prince of Wales and earl of Chester in 1301; the practice of combining these titles has continued right down to the present holder, Prince Charles, and emphasises the close link between Chester and Wales.

Throughout the medieval period Chester remained as much a stronghold of strategic military importance as it had been under the Romans. The ever-present threat of the Welsh waxed and waned according to the strength or weakness of their princes, from the 8th century, when the Mercian King Offa built the great dyke to keep out the dispossessed Welsh of Gwynedd, Powys and Gwent, to the 15th, when Henry Tudor, a Welshman, became king of England. There was a curious occasion in the 10th century when the Saxon King Edgar was rowed in state on the Dee at Chester by a crew which consisted entirely of Celtic princes, in symbolic, even kindly, token of their bondage and allegiance. (The park on the south side of the Old Dee Bridge is known as Edgar's Field – see Walk 4.) The Norman period witnessed the building of the extensive series of border ('Marcher') castles, of which the one at Hawarden (see p. 81) is almost within sight of Chester, and under Edward I there was war (1277 and 1282), resulting in the death of the powerful Welsh Prince Llewellyn and the final conquest of North Wales. Much of the fierce action of the revolt led by Owen Glendower between 1400 and 1412 took place along the border near the Dee, and in North Wales; one of Owen's staunchest generals, his cousin Rhys ap Tudur, was executed in Chester in 1412.

Even so, the city prospered in relative security both as an administrative centre and as the principal port of the whole north-west coast, trading with Ireland, France and Spain. Hugh Lupus ordered the building of the first causeway in the river, which is thought to have been specially designed as a water race for the first mills. The mills were to remain famous for centuries to come – infamous, too, on account of extortion. A succession of powerful owners, first the earls of Chester and, later, members of some prominent local families, would rent the mills at exorbitant rates to individual millers, who in their turn exacted and retained high fees from the farmers who were forced by virtual monopoly to bring their corn here. The city authorities acquired the mills only a short time before they were finally demolished in 1910.

**9** *Hawarden castle, a 13th-century fortress, was one of the line of 'Marcher' castles built along the Welsh border. It was besieged during the Civil War, taken for Charles I and retaken by Cromwell's forces. An 18th-century house near these ruins later became the home of William Gladstone, four times prime minister between 1868 and 1894.*

A wooden bridge over the Dee was destroyed by flooding in 1227, and thereafter replaced several times, until the present stone bridge was built in the late 14th century. By this time the medieval walls were already complete. All this construction work contributed (along with natural erosion and tidal interaction) to the gradual silting of the river, so that by the end of the 1500s the port was no longer viable – a sadly familiar example of sawing away the branch on which you are sitting.

At this period there were nine parishes in the city, besides several religious houses, and two hospitals founded by Earl Ranulph III, a figure of considerable importance whose power and influence had helped John attain the crown on the death of Richard I in 1119.

The Rows, Chester's most characteristic and outstanding feature, unique in Britain, are known to have existed as far back as the 13th century, although they seem to have attracted little attention before the 16th century. Various theories have been devised to account for these rambling arcades all along the main streets and to explain the fact that they are at first floor level in front but at ground level at the rear. This can be seen by walking along Godstall Lane from St Werburgh Street at ground level to the steep flight of steps down to Eastgate Street. In the case of the former Row in Lower Bridge Street, it is simply an effect of geography, as the street runs in a valley, but in other central streets it seems that the Rows may have been constructed in front of spoil heaps, the accumulated detritus of centuries, mixed in with Roman ruins whose stones would have been impossible to shift. Some archaeologists have suggested that the combination of workshops and living quarters with the continuous gallery may be a direct legacy of a Roman pattern of domestic building; another more fanciful proposal is that the streets themselves were excavated in Roman times from the relatively soft underlying red sandstone. Nor is anything certain known about the original purpose of the medieval stone undercrofts or crypts, which are incorporated in several of the street-level shops; most probably they were used as workshops or for storage.

Archaeological study of the Rows began in the early 19th century, and took a great leap forward in 1948 with the establishment of the city's Record Office. Actual excavation is rarely possible in streets where property is variously owned and has prime commercial value, so it seems likely that conflicting theories will have to remain untested and inconclusive. But we can be certain that these continuous galleries have always provided a compact and lively setting for every kind of commercial activity, more vivid in the days when there were stalls against the balustrades, shops at the back of the Rows, workshops below and houses above.

Trades and craft guilds flourished in many towns during the Middle Ages, and more than twenty were already established in Chester towards the end of the 16th century. Unlike a modern trade union a guild embraced everyone involved in its trade, masters as well as workers and apprentices. It aimed to create a monopoly and exercised rigid controls, but its paternalistic stance also involved strong religious connections and charitable activities.

The enduring legacy of the local guilds is the Chester cycle of Mystery Plays, which is one of the glories of English medieval literature. The plays were performed every summer, at Whitsun, and each guild was required to produce a play, which would tour the city on a mobile platform. Biblical scenes from the Creation to the Last Judgement were vigorously enacted, with

**10** *Bishop Lloyd's House, Watergate Street, is considered by many to be the finest black and white building in the city. George Lloyd was Bishop of Chester between 1605 and 1615 and the house is dated 1615. It has two gables and an abundance of fine carving on the exterior panels, especially on the right-hand side. These heraldic beasts and biblical scenes are best appreciated from the Row opposite, and if possible with binoculars. The windows were restored as part of T. M. Lockwood's restoration work (1899). The interior can be seen by arrangement with the tourist information centre; it has an 18th-century Chippendale staircase and fine rooms with plasterwork ceilings, which are now used for meetings of local societies.*

a serious religious and educational purpose, but providing abundant entertainment in the process. Noah has to struggle with his wife, who wants to stay at home and have nothing to do with his new-fangled ark – 'gett thee a newe wyfe', she cries, and it takes the rest of the scene for Noah and his sons to get her on board. The shepherds on their way to Bethlehem share a hearty feast:

> Here is bredd this daye was bacon, [baked]
> onion, garlycke, and leekes,
> butter that bought was in Blacon,
> and greene cheese to greese well your cheekes

(not to mention pudding, an oat cake from Lancashire, and a sheep's head soused in ale, 'a noble supper'). The plays are no longer presented annually, but there have been some powerful and moving revivals, notably one in 1992 directed by Bob Cheeseman.

As the city gained commercial strength its relations with the County Palatine became increasingly strained and in 1506 a charter of Henry VII made Chester an independent county; a few years later it received the right to send two representatives to parliament. The creation of the diocese in 1541 added a new hierarchy to those of army, squirarchy and judiciary (based in the castle), extending and diversifying social life – a situation which still exists today.

*11 The King Charles or Phoenix Tower is the most complete of a series of towers which formed part of the city's defences in the Middle Ages. A phoenix, the emblem of the Guild of Painters, Glaziers, Embroiderers and Stationers, which used to meet here, is still to be seen carved in stone over both doorways. The building was much restored in the 19th century, but the octagonal lower room is medieval.*

18

## Rebellion and Reform

Chester was particularly severely affected by the Civil War because the city supported the king and the county supported parliament. It was besieged for two years, from 1644 to 1646, and suffered considerably in the cause of its less than grateful sovereign. Charles is said to have watched the defeat of his army from the Phoenix (later called the King Charles) Tower (**11**) on the eastern wall north of the cathedral, and then escaped into Wales, leaving the city to starve.

This was an agonising time. The strength of royalist support is scarcely surprising, since the earls of Chester had been active and influential ever since the title was joined to that of prince of Wales in 1301 and, more immediately, the city was indebted to the crown for its independence and power in matters of law enforcement and taxation (and, one need hardly add, wealth). Almost all the prominent families supported the King, who is supposed to have stayed with the Gamulls at Gamull (now Gamul) House in Lower Bridge Street during his visits to Chester in 1642 and 1645. The royalist cause must have been mightily proclaimed from church pulpits, as the appointment of preachers was in the hands of the city fathers, the mayor and aldermen. But an opposing faction was led by a merchant, William Edwards, supported by the common councilmen; puritan books and broadsheets were printed in the city, and contact was maintained with puritan preachers in the county. Sir William Brereton was the parliamentary leader throughout the siege. He had

been deputy lieutenant and member of parliament for Cheshire, and was a man of the deepest conviction and outstanding organising ability, a crucial matter in maintaining support from surrounding counties and from London.

The King first visited Chester in September 1642, a month after the war had begun, and the following winter saw great preparations of inner and outer defences. Brereton attacked in July 1643, and was repulsed; his army was driven out of North Wales by fresh royalist forces brought from Ireland and quartered in Chester. Their presence compounded the city's troubles and a royal proclamation had to be issued against plundering. The siege itself did not begin until the winter of the following year. By the summer of 1645, after the defeat at Naseby, the relief of Chester had become the King's prime concern. He arrived on 23 September and on the following day his army was defeated within sight of the city walls at Rowton Moor, with losses of two thousand men.

The worst hardships came in the winter of 1645–6. Sporadic but fierce bombardment combined with an ever tightening blockade to weaken the morale of the starving populace and garrison and they finally surrendered on 3 February 1646. At this moment the city's governor, John, Lord Byron, wrote that he and his family had 'but half a brown loaf and four biscuits'.

Reorganisation was long and difficult, and a further disaster hit the city in 1647 when a particularly virulent form of plague broke out, killing more than

**13** *A junction of the Shropshire Union Canal, beside the road from Tarporley to Nantwich. The left branch leads to Chester and Ellesmere Port, the right to Birmingham and also into Wales, and the one straight ahead to Middlewich and the Mersey. All canal bridges have a special character, and this one is particularly elegant.*

**14** *Looking from the walls across the green to Abbey Street. The houses belong to the latter half of the 18th century.*

a fifth of the inhabitants. This was not the first time plague had struck Chester, for at least ten outbreaks are recorded over the preceding century and a half; indeed, in 1517, 'many fled so that the grass did grow a foot high near to the High Cross'. The final epidemics, in 1650 and 1661, were milder.

However, the new spirit of civic improvement was abroad, and by the mid 18th century the population numbered around 15,000 and enjoyed a clean and healthy city, with an excellent water supply pumped from the River Dee. Something of this new spirit is exemplified by John Wilkins, Bishop of Chester between 1668 and 1673, who was a distinguished scientist and one of the founders of the Royal Society. He invented a perpetual motion machine, which (according to Geoffrey Taylor in an article in the *Guardian*, 17 June 1985) 'was so sublime that if God had been on the side of the bishops, it would surely have worked. It relied on an endless belt wound round a series of pulleys. Attached to the belt were sponges which entered a bath of water. The wet sponges then weighed more than the dry sponges on the other side of the belt and therefore caused the belt to move. They then had the water pressed out of them at the same time as the dry sponges on the other side of the system were absorbing water from the same bath. The system failed only because more energy was needed to expel the water from the sponges than was delivered by the rotation of the belt.' Surely the bishop must have been motivated by a concern for the practical problems of the diocese, rather than by a desire to refute the second law of thermodynamics? It is sad that he has no memorial in the cathedral.

The number of well-built 18th-century houses, the amount of silver

treasure of this period belonging to the churches, and the elegant marble monuments in churches and in the cathedral are all signs that the city was settling into quiet country-town prosperity. The **Bluecoat School** (**12**; see p. 44) was built in 1717; houses in Abbey Square (**49**), Abbey Street (**14**) and Boughton between 1754 and 1828; 'one of the best Georgian houses' (Pevsner), Greenbank in Eaton Road, between 1812 and 1825. Further indications of the city's improved fortunes are the shot tower (just north of the canal, near the station), which processed lead from nearby mines at Holywell (see p. 82) from the end of the 18th century, and the lavish extension of the castle, in Greek Revival style, between 1788 and 1822.

Chester had long been noted for its manufacture and export of leather goods. Dutch settlers carried on a small textile industry and clay tobacco pipes were made locally. The famous Cheshire cheese was, and remains to this day, a prized commodity. Daniel Defoe in his *Tour* refers to Chester's 'excellent cheese, which they make here in such quantities, and so exceeding good, that as I am told from very good authority, the city of London only take off 14000 ton every year'. It was also sent by river to Bristol and York and shipped from Liverpool to Ireland and Scotland. In addition to these developments in manufacturing, there was considerable growth in the tourist trade, with a great number of inns serving coach traffic to London and elsewhere, and, most importantly, to Liverpool (and thence overseas). These

**15** *The former Grosvenor Club in Vicar's Lane, seen from Grosvenor Park. Chester has a good number of fine mid-18th-century houses like this one, though many were demolished in the Victorian enthusiasm (encouraged by Ruskin) for half-timber revival. This house was once the vicarage of St John's church. The rear of the site has seen some interesting new office development.*

inns also catered for gentry and farming people who came in from the country to pursue business, lawsuits or entertainment. The walls were gradually converted from battlements into a promenade, and the Roodee was devoted to recreation.

The ocean-going trade declined from the 15th century onwards; as early as 1445 it was noted that because of silting no merchant ship could approach within 12 miles of the city, and it gradually became necessary to establish 'havens' lower down the Dee. This problem was compensated for, to some extent, by the growth of internal waterways. In 1735–6 the river was canalised, once more enabling ships, for a time, to reach Chester's ancient quays. But silting continued relentlessly, and the little downstream port of Connah's Quay grew in importance, though it remained small by comparison with Liverpool. The second surge of canal building at the end of the 1700s linked Chester (via the Shropshire Union Canal, constructed between 1779 and 1833) with Wolverhampton and Birmingham in one direction, and in the other with Ellesmere Port, from where passengers could proceed by packet boat for Liverpool and onwards to North America. In 1824 a proposal for linking Manchester to the Dee came to nothing – probably just as well for Chester. Manchester had to wait another 70 years for its ship canal to the Mersey and the open sea, an inestimable commercial blessing even if not a scenic one. The sea-going interest continued almost into the 20th century, when small commercial vessels were still being built in yards near Tower Wharf, and were given a Chester registration.

The world's first boat lift (**16**) was planned and built at Anderton, near

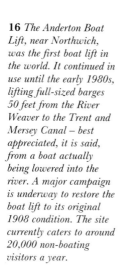

**16** *The Anderton Boat Lift, near Northwich, was the first boat lift in the world. It continued in use until the early 1980s, lifting full-sized barges 50 feet from the River Weaver to the Trent and Mersey Canal – best appreciated, it is said, from a boat actually being lowered into the river. A major campaign is underway to restore the boat lift to its original 1908 condition. The site currently caters to around 20,000 non-boating visitors a year.*

Northwich, during the later 1870s, and has continued in use until recently. It lifted boats 50 feet from the River Weaver to the Trent and Mersey Canal. Another nostalgic sight from the heyday of British canals in this area is near Chirk, south of Wrexham, where the Llangollen Canal passes over the dramatic Pontcysyllte Viaduct.

Railways superseded canals. Pevsner considers Chester's Italianate station (**17**) to be one of the most splendid of the earlier ones. Built in 1847–8, it inspired Thomas Hughes, writing his *Stranger's Handbook to Chester* shortly after, to four pages of delighted rapture: 'What think you . . . of our noble STATION, with its elegant iron roof of sixty foot span, and its thirteen miles of railway line? . . . Stretching away on either side of us, as far as the eye can reach, we see the passengers' arrival and departure sheds, booking offices, refreshment rooms, goods and carriage depots, waterworks, gasworks, and all the other facilities and conveniences which are the usual characteristics of the railway system; while beyond the limits of the Station, . . . the busy hum of life is ceaselessly heard spreading itself in every direction, and rapidly transforming the region of the plough into the turmoil of the town.'

Despite such enthusiasm, which must have been widely shared, the industrial revolution stopped, so far as Chester was concerned, at the station. Great manufacturing towns developed elsewhere, and Chester escaped industrial unrest, although the county did not. In 1811–12 the Cheshire Commission passed 14 death sentences on Luddites (bands of workers in northern England who smashed the machines which deprived them of their livelihood), and two of these were not repealed.

From 1850 onwards energies were directed towards commercial building in the city centre, in styles following the popular vogue for medieval revival. Contemporary methods made possible the construction of buildings of far larger dimensions than had ever been thinkable in the Middle Ages, and they were usually of very high quality. But the fashion also resulted in the

**17** *The railway station, built in 1847–8, is considered one of the best from this early period of the railways. Thomas Hughes (a native of Chester, and remembered now as the author of* Tom Brown's Schooldays) *devotes several excited pages of his* Stranger's Handbook to Chester *to the station and its amenities: 'If you would enjoy an invigorating cup of coffee, unimpeachable pastry, a good glass of ale, or a fragrant cigar, take a turn in the* REFRESHMENT ROOM, *and the utmost wish of your soul will be incontinently gratified.' Alas for the unimpeachable pastries of yesteryear. A major project of renovation and refurbishment of Chester station was begun in 1991.*

*18 These chemical works, part of the industrial landscape beside the Mersey near Runcorn, are a splendid sight after dark, always brilliantly lit. Industrial growth in this part of Cheshire has been formidable, particularly in the chemical and oil industries, but it co-exists peacefully with the long-established farming communities.*

destruction of many 18th-century buildings, which were not appreciated at the time: Mrs Gaskell refers disparagingly to the 'flat, mean, unrelieved style of George III'. The imposing town hall (**46**) was built by W. H. Wynn in 1864–9 in late-13th-century style, and the cathedral was restored by a succession of able and fashionable architects, including Thomas Harrison, R. C. Hussey, Sir George Gilbert Scott and Sir A. W. Blomfield. Much of the activity was instigated by the Duke of Westminster, the ubiquitous landlord of both city and county.

A wedding in the 17th century had had far-reaching consequences. Sir Thomas Grosvenor of Eaton (a village south of Chester) married Mary Davies, heiress to the Ebury estate in London (modern Belgravia and Mayfair), thereby laying the foundation of perhaps the greatest fortune in England. Two years later, in 1679, he was elected as member of parliament for Chester and from the late 17th century the Grosvenors were closely involved in the political and social life of the city. Between 1715 and 1874 the Grosvenor family provided at least one of Chester's MPs and often both. The private Eaton estate, family home of dukes of Westminster to the present day, has seen a succession of houses, none more enchanting than the palace in 'Strawberry Hill Gothick' built between 1803 and 1812, a fairy-tale of delicate pinnacles and fan-vaulting. Alterations to this were started in the 1850s, and a few years later it was totally obliterated by the vast mansion designed by Alfred Waterhouse for the first duke. Pevsner describes this as Wagnerian, 'an outstanding expression of High Victorian originality'. Little remains now, after devastation by fire, and army occupation in the second world war, apart from the clock tower and some stable buildings; the modern ducal residence, built in the 1960s, is a monument of 20th-century bleakness. Nevertheless, the elaborate garden and estate buildings bear witness to the presence of designers and architects such as Capability Brown and Edwin Lutyens. The River Dee flows through the Eaton estate and still to be seen, by boat up-river from Chester, or along the footpath from the village of Aldford, is a graceful single-span bridge (1824), cast by the great iron founder William Hazeldine. The grounds of Eaton Hall are occasionally opened for charity, as on 'Daffodil Sunday', at Easter, and afford some of the best views of the Dee.

During the 20th century Chester has developed in much the same way as country towns elsewhere in England, with extensive though undistinguished suburbs, but the city centre is remarkable for the architectural invention and the careful preservation of buildings of all periods, which are described in greater detail in the walks outlined below. In 1992 the population was about 120,000. The city is a favoured shopping centre drawing on an area extending far beyond the county, into North Wales and southwards into Staffordshire. Vast industries (oil refineries, chemical plants and a motor-car works) have grown up close by, in the Wirral, Ellesmere Port, Runcorn and Northwich – but they have not spoiled Chester's unique and separate identity.

## Conservation

The modern city of Chester has a distinguished and exemplary conservation record, particularly over the last fifteen years. In February 1970 Chester's consultant architect, Donald Insall, presented a report on his pilot study, 'Action for Conservation', and in the same year Chester was the first city in Britain to appoint a conservation officer. More recently, in 1982, it was the first local authority to win the European Prize for the Preservation of Historic Monuments, a prize which had only come to Britain once before. Two years later the city was presented with the Europa Nostra Medal for its outstanding achievements in the Bridgegate area.

**19** *The River Dee may no longer be suitable for ocean-going vessels but it is enjoyed by fishermen, even in a dank and dark December. The Groves make a very different picture in the summer months, when they are animated by visitors and pleasure boats.*

**20** *Stanley Palace, dating from 1591, was built by Peter Warburton, a lawyer and MP for Chester. It became the town house of the powerful Stanley of Alderley family through the marriage of Warburton's daughter to Sir Thomas Stanley. The Stanleys' kinsmen, the earls of Derby, controlled the nearby Watergate and levied tolls on all goods and people entering Chester. Eventually Stanley Palace passed to them. In 1828 it was given to the city by the Earl of Derby and since then it has been extensively restored from a derelict condition. At one time there was a suggestion that it should be reconstructed in the United States. It is currently occupied by the English Speaking Union, and is open to visitors. Another former town house of a great local family is now The Falcon, on the corner of Lower Bridge Street and Grosvenor Street; this belonged to the Grosvenors.*

Insall's report stressed that 'in an historic city, we must define the chief attractions, then work within them to release the potential of every under-used asset. In this way the whole can become again a single, balanced and thriving entity.' He examined succinctly, yet in some detail, the current state of the Rows, the city walls, the cathedral precinct and King Street, and assessed the risks of inaction. He applauded the newly completed Grosvenor shopping precinct: 'Busy new shops have been stitched into the heart of a whole island of property at the same level as the upper Row, with gentle gradients and heated pavements. By utilizing the natural fall of the land, the whole is serviced from below.' He made a realistic appraisal of the costs of conservation, and recommended a phased programme. The first year would instigate first-aid to arrest galloping decay in 28 listed buildings, and an 'early-warning care' system for further groups of buildings; in the first five years 142 historic buildings would be repaired and converted; the next decade would deal with 229 more.

The report was warmly received and the programme was immediately adopted. The Cestrians themselves make a contribution towards the costs, since a penny rate is allocated specifically for conservation. In addition to the £200,000 per annum raised in this way, there has been considerable help from central government, while grant-aided private developers and housing societies have played an essential part. Progress has been dramatic, particularly in the areas of the Bridgegate in the south and King Street in the north, both of which were virtually derelict in 1970. The improvements are not only aesthetic, for they have enhanced property values and provided more housing within the city.

One example of the complexity of the problems encountered in the conservation programme is Bridgegate House, in the centre of Bridge Place

(**22**), a fine Georgian terrace in Lower Bridge Street. In addition to the dilapidation caused by years of disuse, it was discovered that its rear walls were founded on the remains of a Roman quarry, resting partly on solid rock and partly on a rubbish dump, necessitating the extensive underpinning of the whole building. The work was first taken in hand by Cheshire County Council, and more recently the property has been developed privately, to include a small restaurant, office and residential accommodation, and preserving the Georgian staircase and a Roman well. All this has been helped by a grant from the Historic Buildings and Monuments Commission.

Gamul House, on the opposite side of Lower Bridge Street, was in an even worse state of disrepair, and has been beautifully restored. As in many instances throughout the city, meticulous attention has been given to recording all the discoveries made in this Jacobean house: for example, a quantity of medieval floor tiles was found in the roof, where they had been used as builders' rubble; they are now on display in the hall.

Efforts have not been limited to the larger houses: the Albion Street scheme renovated Victorian terraces to provide lower-income housing, as can be seen from the walls in Walk 2. The project was completed in 1988 and some of the houses involved presented unusually difficult problems of access to hitherto unoccupied and neglected upper floors. It has not always been possible to bring fire escapes into line with present-day regulations, and the City Council has had to remain content with making the best of a bad job, as in one case in Watergate Row, where the escape route entails climbing out of a back window, clambering over a roof to a windowsill

**21** *Heritage Court, Lower Bridge Street. Conservation work by the architects Forbes Bramble Associates has produced a shop and office development of considerable elegance, with alternating brick and plaster façades looking onto a brick-paved courtyard. The 17th-century street front over the entrance archway has been carefully and successfully reconstructed.*

with a brick on it, breaking the window with the brick, and then getting through the window into a warehouse and down into a back alley.

Modern pedestrianisation schemes and an effective system of bus routes and car parks inside the city walls help to alleviate traffic congestion and make a walk through the city relaxed and pleasurable. Even the ground under the visitor's feet has not been forgotten: unsightly tarmac has been replaced by setts and stone paving, and further work is planned for the use of such traditional materials in Northgate Street near the Forum. The restored 18th-century cobbles of Abbey Street (see Walk 2) are probably the only listed street surface in England.

**22** *These handsome Georgian houses, Nos. 7, 9 and 11 Lower Bridge Street, are part of Bridge Place, a terrace set back from the road near the Bridgegate.*

# Four Walks through the City

## Walk 1: Eastgate Street, Watergate Street and Bridge Street

It has been suggested that each of the central streets should be walked four times, in each direction at ground level, and then again at Row level. We do not aim to be quite so exhaustive, or exhausting.

The Cross (**24**) is the hub of the city, and has been ever since the Romans laid out their rectangular street plan, with administrative headquarters at the intersection, where St Peter's church now stands. This church dates from the 1300s, and against its walls was erected a two-storey wooden building, the Pentice (a pent-house, i.e. adjoining structure), which remained the civic centre and court-house for several centuries. It was removed in 1803 to improve access to Northgate Street. The Cross itself was erected on the present site in 1407, demolished in the Civil War, reconstructed in the 'Roman Garden' (see p. 54) from fragments found near St Peter's, and brought back to the city centre in 1975, when this area was freed from motor traffic – a happy improvement, although as yet the civic authorities have not seen fit to replace the fountain which used to flow with wine on festive occasions. St Peter's is much restored, and unusual in that what remains is almost square in plan, with four aisles, galleries and green-painted pews; it has the good atmosphere of a working church.

Starting from the Cross (a sandstone pillar, not actually cross-shaped), and taking the Row on the right of Eastgate Street (the south side), the first visit should be to the jewellers' shop, Mappin and Webb (**4**), where they are pleased to show their Jacobean (or Oak) Room. This has a fine carved mantelpiece depicting a rural scene and view of the port of Chester and the Old Dee Bridge, dated 1664. Jewellers have always occupied these premises, and the window of this room has stained-glass coats of arms of some of the previous proprietors, including that of Richard Richardson, who in 1707 controlled the Assay Office, where gold and silver were tested. (The Chester Assay Office, sited in various places since then, closed in 1962, and so silver produced in the city no longer bears the Chester hallmark – an erect sword between three wheatsheaves, as shown on the 18th-century glass goblet (**30**) in the Grosvenor Museum.)

Next door to Mappin and Webb's is Browns of Chester, where the superb medieval crypt has been converted into a restaurant. In the mid 19th century T. M. Penson designed the High Victorian Gothic Crypt Buildings, to the right of the slightly earlier Classical shopfront, to harmonise with the crypt beneath. The third part of Browns' shopfront, to the left of the Classical Building, was also designed by Penson and is one of the earliest examples of the half-timber revival. Penson practised in Chester and was known chiefly for

the part he played in this revival. He was also responsible for the Norman-style chapel in the cemetery south of Grosvenor Bridge and the east window of St John's church (see Walk 4). Over the street from here are some of the smaller 19th-century black and white restorations, notably The Boot, and the building above Moss Bros the tailors (**23**) – particularly elaborate, with bays and alcoves and barley-sugar columns. Compare this with the exterior of Mappin and Webb's, seen from the so-called 'Dark Row' on the north side of the street, where the timber frame is an integral part of the structure, and altogether simpler.

**23** *This particularly ornate example of Victorian half-timbering, which has barley sugar columns and little alcoves, is on the north side of Eastgate Street and contrasts with the severly neo-classical and unlovable bank on the right, erected in 1860 by George Williams.*

**24** *The Cross stands at the heart of the city, where the four main streets meet to form a staggered crossroads. These buildings on the corner of Eastgate Street and Bridge Street, designed by T. M. Lockwood in 1888, are typical of the bravura of Victorian half-timber revival: structurally complex, without excessive ornament, and preserving the Rows and their attractive white-painted balustrades. The street crossing is now entirely free of motor traffic. The Cross itself, on the left in this picture, stood here in the Middle Ages, and was broken up at the time of the Civil War; later the fragments were discovered, reassembled, and placed in the Roman Garden (see p. 54). It was brought back 'home' in 1975. The lantern head of the top section may date from the 14th century, when the little niches would have contained religious statuettes.*

It is hard to imagine that before 1850 this street was characterised by Georgian brick. A walk through the last section of the dim and narrow north Row, which brings us out at the bottom end of Northgate Street, will make it obvious why this was called the 'Dark Row' or the 'Dark Lofts' in Tudor and early Stuart times. It makes a sharp contrast with the bright wide shopping arcade of the south Row.

Passing across Northgate Street and in front of St Peter's church, we come to Watergate Street, which has a wide range of building styles, including Rows on the south side as far as Weaver Street and on the north side as far as Crook Street, more crypts than any other street in the city, one exceptionally handsome Georgian house (the Booth Mansion, Nos. 28–34), and several fine examples of 17th-century black and white. The first of these, on the left, is God's Providence House (**25**), originally built in 1652 but reconstructed by James Harrison in 1862. The inscription 'God's Providence is Mine Inheritance' is believed to refer to the plague which struck Chester in the late 1640s, after the Civil War siege, and to the fact that the owner of this house escaped the infection. Its timber frame creates a square pattern, and the spaces between are decorated with ornamental plasterwork, or pargetting.

A few steps along on the same side, at Row level, is the Leche House, the town house of a county family of that name (it is now a furniture shop). It is not heavily restored, so gives perhaps the best impression to be found in this whole area of an Elizabethan domestic interior. Some of the walls are thickly plastered, but attractively picked out in colour. The hall, which is two storeys high, is dominated by a large fireplace (**27**) surmounted by the Leche family coat of arms, and beside the chimney there is a hiding place which is thought to have been a priest's hole. High in the wall to the right of the fireplace, and clearly seen from the wavering floor-boards of the open gallery, is a curious and unexplained peephole.

Bishop Lloyd's House (**10**), dated 1615, towards the end of the Row on the south side, is Chester's finest early-17th-century house. (Application for viewing the interior should be made at the tourist information centre.) It also has an 18th-century Chippendale staircase, and a range of handsome rooms with stucco ceilings. The exterior, with its two big gables, is best seen from the Row on the opposite side of the street, and it is worth taking binoculars to examine the small carved panels of biblical subjects: Abraham, on the point of sacrificing his son Isaac, appears as a Jacobean gentleman, with bulbous breeches and puffed sleeves, all embroidered.

Near the end of the street, on the right, the Guildhall is a conversion of a 19th-century church, and one example of the practical and constructive use which Chester has made of several deconsecrated churches. Opposite is the Custom House Inn (1657), which has been greatly restored during the course of this century. On the corner of Watergate Street and Nicholas Street (part of the new ring road) is the Axe Tavern, on the site of the former Yacht Inn. This was where Dean Swift (author of *Gulliver's Travels*) once stayed. He was so offended by some cathedral dignitaries' having refused his invitation to dine, that he left a verse scratched on a window with his diamond ring:

> Rotten without and mouldering within,
> This place and its clergy are both near akin.

A few minutes' walk south along Nicholas Street brings us to Grosvenor

**25** *God's Providence House, Watergate Street, dates from 1652 and was rebuilt in 1862, when a public outcry prevented its demolition and persuaded the owner to restore it in traditional style, using some of the original timbers. The Row was raised to match the level of its neighbours, the windows were enlarged, and the decorative plasterwork (pargetting), not seen elsewhere in Chester, was added at the same time.*

OVERLEAF

**26** *The galleries known as the Rows are one of the hallmarks of Chester, and unique in Britain. Watergate Street, shown here, has Rows on either side, as do Eastgate Street and Bridge Street. The origin and purpose of these arcades are still not known for certain, and make a focus for continuing archaeological investigation. Chester must have been a wonderfully lively place when families lived in these high, narrow properties, and plied all manner of trades.*

GODS·PROVIDENCE·IS·MINE·INHERITANCE

Street, where we cross the road to the Grosvenor Museum, one of whose founders was Charles Kingsley. Famous as the author of *The Water Babies* and *Westward Ho*, he was also president of the Chester Society of Natural Science in 1871, and at that time a canon of the cathedral. T. M. Lockwood designed the building in free Renaissance style with Dutch gables, continuing the turrets and ornament of the slightly earlier Trustee Savings Bank next door. The bank, by the Chester architect James Harrison, winner of a competition for the best Tudor-style design, is unfortunately built in the stark and uncompromising red Ruabon brick which so delighted builders in Cheshire and all along the Welsh border because of the way it withstands weathering. Inside the museum there is a very handsome curving staircase with cast-iron bannisters. The atmosphere is unusually friendly.

In the century since its foundation the museum has been a centre for archaeological study: its importance has increased greatly in recent years along with the growing general popularity of archaeology, and also thanks to its many pertinent publications and discussion papers. The Roman Stones Gallery, already mentioned, is complemented by a second room with pictorial reconstructions of Roman life, and a collection of artefacts and a separate display of archaeology since 1970. A corridor leads to a Georgian town house where there are some vivid and carefully researched Georgian and Victorian interiors. The Kingsley Room on the first floor is the natural history section, and there is an art gallery on the second floor. The modest collection of oils and watercolours covering a period of two centuries (not shown in its entirety)

**27** *The fireplace in Leche House, Watergate Street. The interior of this late-16th-century house is particularly interesting because it is less heavily restored than similar buildings in the city centre. Above the fireplace is the colourful Leche family coat of arms, and to the right is a cavity which may have been a priests' hole (a hiding place for persecuted Catholics in Elizabethan times).*

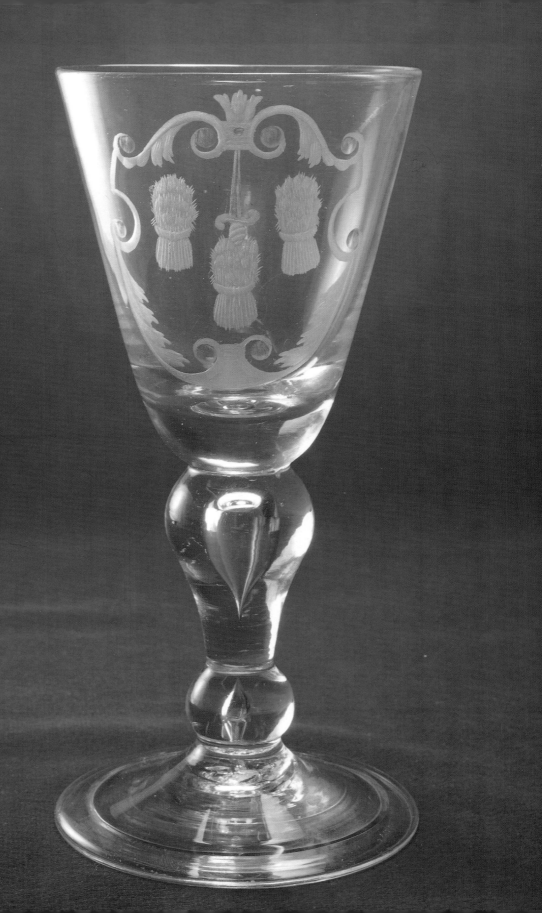

PREVIOUS PAGE

**28** *St Michael's Buildings dominate Bridge Street, halfway down on the east side. They were completed in 1910, and the original white-tiled facing attracted so much criticism that the second duke of Westminster ordered it to be changed to the black and white we see today. But tiles were retained in St Michael's Arcade, which runs in from the Row at right angles.*

**29** *The 13th-century crypt of Quellyn Roberts' (wine merchants), in Watergate Street (not always open for public viewing). There are several other remarkably well-preserved medieval crypts in the central area of the city, and two can be seen in normal shopping hours: 12 Bridge Street (currently a bookshop) and 28 Eastgate Street (Browns' crypt restaurant).*

**30** *One of the treasures of the Grosvenor Museum: an early-18th-century glass goblet engraved with the old Chester City coat of arms. The new one, divided in two with the three leopards added on the left-hand side was officially granted in 1580 but was not used until the late 18th century.*

has considerable local interest, with scenes by many Chester artists, including Walter Crane and Randolph Caldecott. The valuable record of mid-Victorian Chester in the paintings of Louise Rayner (1829–1924) is of particular note; the watercolours capture the atmosphere of the city streets and illustrate her ability as a draughtsman. Subjects include Bishop Lloyd's House, the Dutch Houses in Bridge Street and the town hall. There are also paintings of Chester attributed to Cotman and De Wint.

From the museum we turn right, cross the road and continue along Grosvenor Street before bearing left into Bridge Street. The narrow road to the left is White Friars, where No. 1 dates from 1648 and is due for some restoration. Bridge Street, by contrast, is proud, prosperous and carefully conserved, and best appreciated from this west side at street level. (We will see the other side in Walk 4.) The Roman south gate would have stood at the present junction of Bridge Street and White Friars. The most striking and dominant feature of Bridge Street is the vast black and white St Michael's Buildings (**28**) of 1910, which also serves as an entrance to St Michael's Arcade, an unusually early example of a covered shopping street on first-floor level, extending back at right angles to the Row; it has been successfully married into the more recent Grosvenor shopping precinct development. St Michael's church, on the corner with Pepper Street, was one of the nine medieval parish churches of Chester, first mentioned in the 12th century. Its oldest remaining parts are the north arcade and the beautiful chancel roof, which dates from the end of the 15th century. The church was largely rebuilt in 1582, enlarged in 1679 and extensively altered and restored in 1849–50 by James Harrison. His replacement of the early-18th-century tower extends beyond the body of the church and the Row passes through it. When the parishes of Chester were reorganised in 1971, St Michael's became redundant and was subsequently bought by Chester City Council and imaginatively converted into the Heritage Centre (see p. 71). In the Row on the west side, which, unlike St Michael's Row, is discontinuous, there is a small, densely packed Toy Museum, of more interest to nostalgic adults than to children. At No. 12 (now a bookshop) is a well-preserved medieval crypt (1270–80), one of several in this area of the city centre and the one that can most readily be seen. The complex turreted building on the south-east corner of the Cross dates from 1888, and was featured on one of the postage stamps issued to commemorate European Architectural Heritage Year in 1975. It was built for the Duke of Westminster by T. M. Lockwood, a Chester architect and a pupil of T. M. Penson. Like Penson he was a leading figure in the black and white revival. Lockwood was also responsible for Nos. 2–4 Bridge Street (1892), on the opposite corner, which combines half-timber with brick and shows Lockwood's typical use of Renaissance ornament and round-headed centre window lights. He also restored Bishop Lloyd's House (**10**) in Watergate Street, seen earlier in this walk.

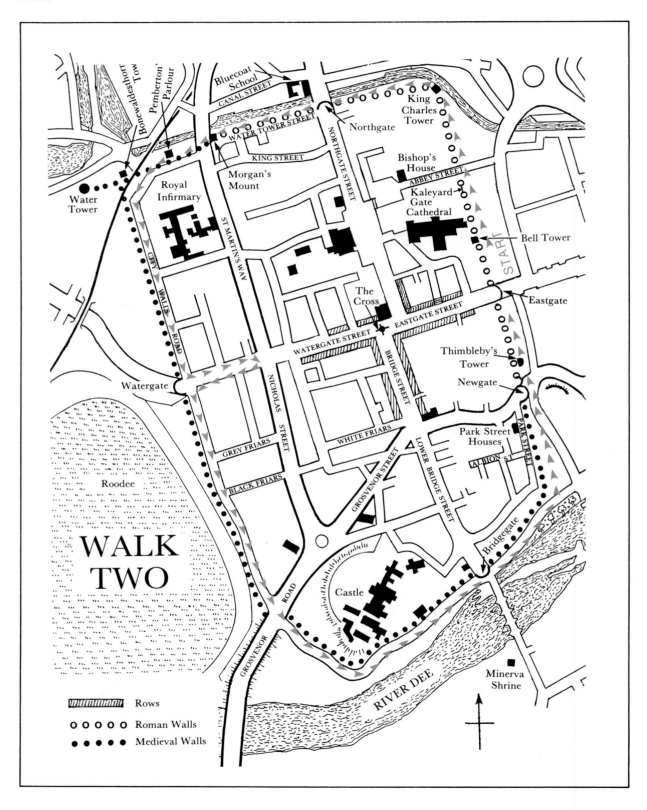

Bonewaldesthorn Tow[er]

Pemberton' Parlour

Bluecoat School

CANAL STREET

King Charles Tower

Northgate

Water Tower

WATER TOWER STREET

KING STREET

NORTHGATE STREET

Bishop's House

ABBEY STREET

Kaleyard Gate

Cathedral

Bell Tower

START

Royal Infirmary

Morgan's Mount

ST MARTIN'S WAY

CITY WALLS ROAD

The Cross

EASTGATE STREET

Eastgate

Thimbleby's Tower

Newgate

WATERGATE STREET

BRIDGE STREET

Watergate

NICHOLAS STREET

WHITE FRIARS

Park Street Houses

PARK STREET

GREY FRIARS

ALBION ST

Roodee

BLACK FRIARS

GROSVENOR STREET

LOWER BRIDGE STREET

# WALK TWO

ROAD

Castle

Bridgegate

GROSVENOR

RIVER DEE

Minerva Shrine

Rows

○○○○○ Roman Walls

●●●●● Medieval Walls

## Walk 2: The City Walls

A walk round the complete two-mile circuit of the walls will take between one and two hours, and access is possible at any of the city's six gates, as well as from City Walls Road and Nuns Road where the walls are no higher than the street level. The eastern half is the more interesting historically, while the western half offers attractive views of the surrounding landscape. There are unique prospects of the city itself, nowhere better than from the Eastgate, under the clock (**31**) which commemorates Queen Victoria's diamond jubilee (1897). From here we can look east along Foregate Street, which follows the direction of the main Roman road from Chester to the north of Britain. The furthest point visible as the road bends away to join City Road is known as The Bars, because in the Middle Ages an outer gate in the city's defences stood there. Immediately to the right, with its entrance in St John's Street, is the Blossoms Hotel, which opened in 1640 and was the terminus for the London–Chester coaches. The London terminus was at St Lawrence Jewry, near the Guildhall in the City; St Lawrence was traditionally depicted surrounded by blossoms, which have remained as this inn's sign to this day. Looking west we see busy Eastgate Street, now happily clear of motor traffic, then the Cross at the central intersection, and then Watergate Street on a slightly downward slope. The great charm of this view is the prospect of open country beyond the Watergate.

If we follow the walls northwards from the Eastgate (i.e. in an anti-clockwise direction) we come first to the new bell tower, and then to the cathedral (see Walk 3). Here we are walking on Roman foundations, and we can see part of them by descending to street level through the new Mercia Square shopping precinct to our right. When we return to the walls the cathedral appears beyond the Cheshire Regiment Memorial Garden, which merges into a green, overlooked by a terrace of mainly 18th-century houses in cobbled Abbey Street (**14**). Where the street meets the walls there is a little tunnel, the Kaleyard Gate, so called because it enabled the monks to get from the monastery to their kale-yards, or kitchen gardens, on the outer side of the walls. Edward I granted permission for the walls to be breached at this point in 1275. The gate is still controlled by the dean and chapter and is closed after 9 p.m.

The impressive tower a few steps along is the King Charles or Phoenix Tower (**11**), which marks the north-east corner of both the Roman and the medieval walls; 'King Charles' because from here King Charles I is said to have watched the defeat of his army at the battle of Rowton Moor on 24 September 1645, and 'Phoenix' because in earlier times this was the meeting place of the Guild of Painters, Glaziers, Embroiderers and Stationers whose emblem was a phoenix. It now houses a tiny museum displaying records and relics of the Civil War.

Again we are directly above some sections of the Roman wall, which are skirted by the canal. Inaugurated in 1722, the Chester Canal was incorporated into the national canal network in the 1830s and became known as the Shropshire Union Canal. The ramparts here are towering and formidable – their height can best be appreciated from George Street on the other side of the canal. On the walls just before we reach the Northgate, No. 1 City Walls has been partially and creatively renovated to house small artisan shops.

The Northgate (**33**) was rebuilt in 1808–10 by Thomas Harrison, commissioned by the first duke of Westminster, who had been elected mayor of Chester in 1807. Unlike the red sandstone Eastgate, Watergate and Bridge-gate, the Northgate is a sombre grey. The former gatehouse was used as a prison and offenders were brought here across the sinister little 'Bridge of Sighs' (now blank at either end), without any parapet or handrail to protect them from what must be a hundred foot drop into the canal. In order to see the bridge we must go down into Upper Northgate Street, as the old gatehouse obscures the view from the walls at this point. Further along Upper Northgate Street is the Bluecoat School (12), one of the best of Chester's 18th-century buildings, founded in 1700 by Bishop Stratford. It is built of brick with stone dressings and has two projecting wings. Although no longer a school, the almshouses within its courtyard, visible from further along the walls, are still in use. They were rebuilt in 1854 but were founded at the beginning of the 13th century by Earl Ranulph III as the hospital of St John the Baptist – for 'poor and feeble men' of Chester. There are 14 entrances in the plain red brick building, where a few geraniums in window boxes do their best to relieve the forbidding grey brick of the courtyard floor.

Returning to the walls at the Northgate we continue westwards towards the new bridge, St Martin's Gate, by which they cross the ring road. Just before this there is a look-out point called Morgan's Mount, named after a Captain Morgan who commanded part of King Charles's defensive garrison. This marks the north-west corner of the Roman wall, which originally followed a line southward, parallel with the new road. The medieval walls, however, continue west at this point, towards the River Dee. If we turn and look towards the city from this vantage point we can see an outstanding example of Chester's enlightened conservation scheme. The elegant Georgian terrace in the foreground, King's Buildings, and the 18th- and 19th-century houses in King Street, which extends eastwards from it, have all been splendidly restored and repaired.

A diversion down the steps beside the road bridge brings us to the canal towpath and the Northgate Locks, with their pretty white-painted ironwork. The deep 'staircase' of three locks, excavated from the sandstone, has a fall of 33 feet; it was built by the Scottish engineer Thomas Telford, who was also responsible for the Ellesmere and Caledonian Canals. To the north of the basin at the lower end of the locks, where the canal meets the River Dee, is Tower Wharf, from which boat trips may be taken along the canal in horse-drawn barges.

On the walls again, we come to the remains of three medieval towers. The first, the Goblin Tower or Pemberton's Parlour (35), was neatly restored in 1874. It bears a plaque commemorating the murengers, the city officials entrusted with maintaining the walls from 1702 onwards. (In 1985 the annual cost of this maintenance was £20,000, and additional grants have to be sought for major repairs.) A half segment remains of the original circular tower, which would have straddled the walls. Next comes the rectangular Bone-waldesthorne's Tower, which marks the north-west corner of the medieval walls. It was actually built in the Dee, but because the river was receding it was necessary to build the New or Water Tower to defend what was then the harbour. This third tower, dating from 1322, is connected to Bonewaldes-thorne's Tower by a battlemented wall of formidable proportions, and together with the long drop on the outside of the walls this forms an impressive

*31 The clock over the Eastgate, seen from the walls: this is one of Chester's most popular landmarks, and was installed to commemorate Queen Victoria's diamond jubilee in 1897. It was made by J. B. Joyce of Whitchurch and stands on an iron turret designed by the Chester architect John Douglas. The gate itself is dated 1768–9, and was erected at the expense of Richard, Lord Grosvenor. From the top of the gate we have the best of the townscape views, with open country at the far end of Watergate Street to the west and the gentle rise of the nearest Welsh hills often clearly visible.*

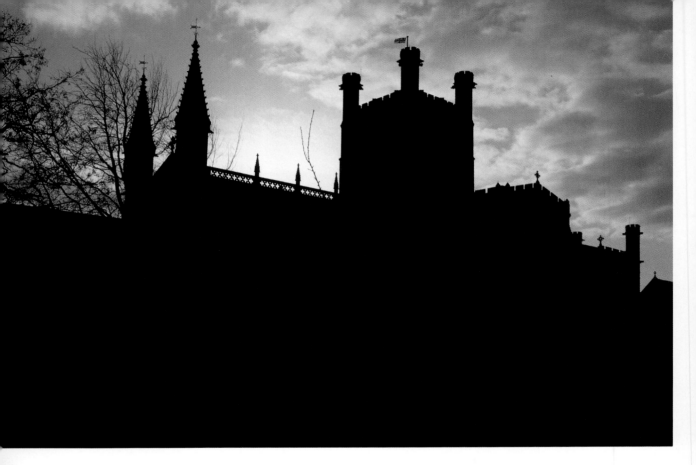

fortification. To our right as we turn south, away from the canal, the scene opens out, with parks and playing fields, and the railway running into North Wales.

The walls now run alongside and on a level with City Walls Road. To our left is the Chester Royal Infirmary. The attractive southernmost part was the first of the buildings, erected in 1761 on the site of the Roman parade ground and cemetery. The hospital was supported by subscriptions and donations, and a patient needed a letter of recommendation from a subscriber in order to be admitted. Here the side streets are lined with Georgian terraces. Sedan House, at the end of Stanley Place, is so named because it boasts the curiosity of a sedan porch, an almost cubic doorway, designed to accommodate a sedan chair and enable the passenger to enter the house without getting cold or wet.

At the Watergate (**36**) we can make a detour down the steps into Watergate Street to see Stanley Palace (**20**), on the right just before the ring road. This handsome half-timbered house dates from the early 17th century, and was the town house of the Stanleys of Alderley. It was extended in 1700 with the addition of the Queen Anne Room, with a fine plastered ceiling displaying the family coat of arms. It has had a chequered history, but was beautifully restored in 1935 (the right-hand gable and the street frontage are clearly recognisable as part of this major renovation). It is now open to public viewing, and used for a variety of functions.

After the Watergate the walls run at street level again. To the left, leading off the opposite side of Nuns Road, are Grey Friars and Black Friars, streets whose names recall the Franciscan and Dominican monastic houses which

**32** *The cathedral at dusk, seen from the walls.*

**33** *The Northgate (1808–10), marking the end of one of the four main Roman streets of the city, was designed by Thomas Harrison, who studied architecture in Italy and practised in Chester for nearly 30 years, being appointed County Surveyor and Bridgemaster in 1815.*

**34** *The Shropshire Union Canal and the city walls, seen from the Northgate: the Roman foundations of the walls are plainly visible. The canal, begun in the 1770s, linked the Midlands to the Mersey ports. This section was part of the original Roman moat.*

46

**35** *Pemberton's Parlour, originally a circular tower on the walls to the west of the Northgate, was rebuilt in the early 18th century, and named after John Pemberton, a mayor of the city; it is also inexplicably known as the Goblin Tower. The plaque commemorates the murengers, the officials who levied a tax for the maintenance of the city walls.*

**37** *Stapleton Cotton, Field Marshal Viscount Combermere (1772–1865), fought in the Napoleonic wars, and served as commander in the West Indies (1817–20), commander-in-chief in Ireland (1822–5) and commander in India (1825–30). This imposing bronze equestrian statue, by the fashionable sculptor Baron Marochetti, was made possible by public subscription. It is strikingly sited on a traffic island between the Roodee and the neo-classical castle entrance.*

**36** *A view through the Watergate (1788) up Watergate Street, towards the centre of Chester. The houses in this part of Watergate Street led up from the quays and shipbuilders' yards outside the city walls.*

ERECTED
IN HONOR OF
STAPLETON COTTON
VISCOUNT COMBERMERE
FIELD MARSHAL

were established there in the 1230s. To the right is Chester's famous racecourse, the Roodee. The name derives from two words, 'rood' meaning cross, and 'eye' meaning island – indicating another religious association and the possibility that there was an island in the Dee at this point. Traces of the Roman harbour have been found here, below the present walls. There are currently three race meetings a year, in May, July and September.

Before we cross the Grosvenor Road we should pause to take in a splendid view of the Dee, spanned by the noble Grosvenor Bridge (**38**) and set against the solid but not inelegant villas of Curzon Park. The prospect from this south-west corner of the city is a varied one: the brilliant green of the Roodee with its reminders of jolly days at the races; the castle, firmly medieval, expansively neo-classical; the bronze statue of Field-Marshal Viscount Combermere, stolidly astride a graceful horse (**37**), his military glories recorded for all to read; the modest Victoriana of the Trustee Savings Bank, the Grosvenor Museum and the church of St Francis. But a powerful effort of imagination is needed to visualise the present townscape as it was before the police headquarters (in the middle distance to our left) came into being. This sore thumb of a building, with sides of solid concrete adorned with an irregular pattern of inverted worm castings, was opened in 1969, and two years later was given a Civic Trust Award, to the bewildered astonishment of all Cestrians.

In order to rejoin the walls we cross the road. What we see of the castle from this side is the stark and uncompromising grimness of its most ancient part, the so-called Agricola Tower (**56**), and it is easy to understand that for many

**38** *The Grosvenor Bridge makes a noble entrance to Chester from Eaton Hall, the Grosvenor family home since the 15th century, and from the Welsh border country. This beautiful segmental arch was designed by Thomas Harrison, who was also responsible for the Greek Revival castle buildings. The bridge was not completed until 1833, after his death, but at that time it was the largest of its kind in the world. The main building material is sandstone from nearby Peckforton.*

centuries it housed a prison. Further along the walls, to the right, the river prospect is delightful, giving us our first sight of the seven irregular arches of the splendid Old Dee Bridge, which dates from 1387 and was a toll bridge until 1885. The unobtrusive electrical power house, on the right just before the bridge, is the site of the famous mill, immortalised in the song 'The Miller of Dee'.

From the Bridgegate we have another interesting view of a city street, this time Lower Bridge Street (see Walk 4), which has received a great deal of sensitive and imaginative restoration over the last ten years. It has some excellent Georgian houses, and several of Chester's finest timbered buildings. Nearest to us on the left hand side of Lower Bridge Street is a generously proportioned inn, The Bear and Billet (**40**), built in 1664. It was originally the town house of the Earl of Shrewsbury, guardian of the Bridgegate. The windows of this inn contain over 1,000 panes of glass.

The walls continue from the Bridgegate as an ever higher footpath, quite separate from the city streets and intriguingly hemmed in by houses, mostly 19th century. There is a long view upriver, taking in the elegant iron suspension bridge (**39**), a footbridge over to the suburb of Queen's Park. The banks on the northern side of the Dee are known as the Groves (**57** and **58**), from where pleasure boats ply in the summer months. The walls now take us north, away from the river, towards the Newgate.

**39** *The elegant suspension bridge leads from the Groves to Queen's Park, a quiet, leafy, mid-Victorian suburb. In his* Stanger's Handbook to Chester *(1856), Thomas Hughes commends the 'salubrity of the air' and the 'beautiful river scenery'. The bridge was first built in 1852 and then rebuilt in 1923.*

**40** *The Bear and Billet public house, Lower Bridge Street, is a fine, relatively late example (1664) of black and white building. Until the mid 19th century it was owned by the earls of Shrewsbury – they had been part custodians of the Bridgegate since the mid 17th century. Goods would have been hoisted through the door in the gable for storage in the attics. The two continuous ranges of windows were probably extended to their present form some time in the 19th century.*

**41** *Part of a row of timber-framed almshouses known as the Park Street Houses, dated 1658, seen from the city walls, south of the Newgate. Six houses remain of the original nine. In the mid 1960s they were uninhabitable and threatened with demolition. A grant from the Historic Buildings Council made their restoration possible – an example of the restrained and sensitive conservation work which has been carried out in Chester since the early 1970s.*

On our left on this last part of the circuit are the so-called Park Street Houses (**41**), a row of gabled almshouses, dated 1658, which were lovingly rescued from almost total dereliction in 1969 (only six of the original nine remain). Next to them, and making an interesting contrast, stands a black and white timbered house built in 1881. It bears on a high beam the motto 'The Fear of the Lord is the Fountain of Life' (said to have been taken from an ancient coin discovered on this site); below this, two windows carry the ominous though possibly less permanent message 'Dental Surgery'. Behind Park Street can be seen the Victorian terraced houses in Albion Street, built in the late 1860s to provide homes for skilled workers, and saved in the last few years from a state of severe neglect.

The 'Roman Garden' (**43**), on the outer side of the walls, is a quiet green which has become the resting place for some fragments of Roman stonework, found during the excavations of Chester, including a small reconstruction of a hypocaust. Hypocausts consisted of a mass of squat stone columns, about two feet high, supporting a floor; hot air was blown between them from a furnace below floor level, providing a form of central heating. (There is a photograph in *Chester as it was*, of an excavation in 1863, which gives an idea of the extent

**42** *The Newgate is modern, completed in 1938 as an early contribution to the projected ring road system. Its strength and colour are in total harmony with the walls, which cross Pepper Street here. There is a good view of the Roman amphitheatre from the Newgate bridge. The oldest city gate, the so-called Wolf Gate, rebuilt in the 1760s, is just to the north of the Newgate.*

**43** *A view from the Newgate of the Roman Garden in springtime. This charming little park is a repository for Roman remains found in the city. These columns come from the legionary baths, and a reconstructed hypocaust can be seen near the top of the picture.*

and sophistication of these constructions.) The entrance to the Roman Garden is at street level, almost under the Newgate.

The Newgate (**42**), a wide stone archway with a tower on either side, is one of two modern gates in the walls; it was designed by Sir Walter and Michael Tapper and built in 1938. Just outside the gate the foundation of the south-east angle-tower of the Roman fortress can be seen. (The second modern gate, more recent still, is St Martin's, on the northern side of Chester, spanning the ring road.) Immediately adjacent to the Newgate (not visible from the walls) is the oldest gate of all, the Wolf Gate. It was rebuilt in the 1760s but had originally been adorned with the coat of arms of Hugh Lupus, nephew of William the Conqueror and earl of Chester. From the top of the Newgate is a view of the Roman amphitheatre, accidentally discovered during building operations, and excavated in the 1960s, and beyond it of St John's church (see Walk 4).

The final monument of our walk along the walls is Thimbleby's Tower, the remains of a watch tower which was heavily damaged during the Civil War siege in 1645, and never rebuilt – in fact it looks more like a well than a tower. A footbridge on the left leads into the new Grosvenor shopping precinct, and from here we rejoin the city streets at the Eastgate.

## Walk 3: Northgate Street and the Cathedral

The southern end of Northgate Street has changed a great deal in the last hundred years. The street-level covered walkway of Shoemakers' Row, on our left as we walk away from the Cross, replaced the original Row, which was demolished at the end of the 19th century. Some of these buildings are probably by John Douglas (1829–1911), the most prolific of the Chester architects involved in the half-timber revival. On the other side of Northgate Street, at No. 12, it is possible to see another fragment of Roman hypocaust (see p. 54) at the back of the shop.

We recross Northgate Street and turn left past The Dublin Packet into narrow Hamilton Place, where there is a small exhibit, behind glass, of the basic stonework of a Roman strongroom, along with a clear plan of the basilica and courtyard which originally occupied this site. This whole segment of the city, between Northgate Street and Watergate Street, was the site of the *principia*, the headquarters complex in the Roman fortress, and has been the scene of intensive archaeological work in recent years, yielding much information about Roman granary and barrack buildings. (Detailed reports on current excavations are issued periodically by the City Council and the Grosvenor Museum.) Hamilton Place abuts on the new Forum shopping centre, and as we continue up Northgate Street we come to the town hall (**46**), in grand Victorian Gothic, reminiscent of St Pancras Station in London. On the same side are the tourist information centre and the public library (**44**), which is a new and particularly successful conversion from an old car works.

With our backs to the library, looking to the right and across the wide top end of St Werburgh Street, we see the west door of the cathedral (**45**) – an unpretentious entrance with a dusty air of disuse. It has medieval carvings of little angels, and a modest Virgin, just discernible. Barclays Bank, the Gothic sandstone building on the corner, was designed by Sir A. W. Blomfield as the King's School in 1876; before this the school, one of Henry VIII's grammar school foundations, had always been housed in the cathedral refectory. It now occupies modern premises on the southern outskirts of Chester.

Further along Northgate Street, on the left past the 1930s cinema, stands The Pied Bull (**47**). Originally called Bull Mansion and the home of the City Recorder in 1533, it was rebuilt in brick in 1654 and became a coaching inn in 1780, when the front was once again rebuilt. A plaque records that George Borrow left from here in 1854 on his tour of 'Wild Wales'. If we cross King Street towards the Northgate we come to a small and ancient house which protrudes into the street. This is The Blue Bell (**48**), which proudly proclaims the date 1494; it is said to be the oldest domestic building in the city, and has narrowly escaped demolition on several occasions. We return down Northgate Street towards the cathedral. Directly opposite the town hall, the low and powerful 14th-century arch of the Abbey Gateway (**2**) brings us into Abbey Square (**49**), the peaceful enclave of the cathedral precinct. Two stone houses, Nos. 13 and 14, erected by Bishop Bridgeman, who was also responsible for the furnishing of the consistory court (see p. 68), are of the 17th century, but the overall appearance is Georgian, self-contained and brick. The cobbles of the square are patterned by 'wheelers' (narrow paved paths which gave carriages a smoother passage); in the central green stands a pillar which is said to have come from the Exchange in Northgate Street – the Corporation's headquarters from the end of the 17th century until it was badly damaged by

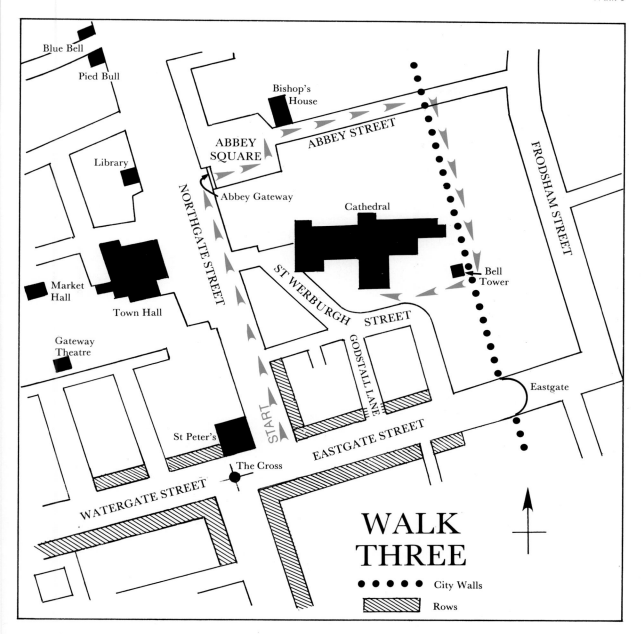

Blue Bell

Pied Bull

Bishop's House

Library

ABBEY SQUARE

ABBEY STREET

FRODSHAM STREET

NORTHGATE STREET

Abbey Gateway

Cathedral

Market Hall

Town Hall

Bell Tower

Gateway Theatre

ST WERBURGH STREET

GODSTALL LANE

Eastgate

START

St Peter's

The Cross

EASTGATE STREET

WATERGATE STREET

# WALK THREE

● ● ● ● ●  City Walls

▨▨▨  Rows

fire in 1862. The unassuming Bishop's House, surrounded by a pretty walled garden, lies on the side opposite the gateway, and from that corner we can make our way along the unworldly cobbles of Abbey Street, and so on to the walls, to have our first proper sight of the cathedral.

Chester cathedral cannot be counted among the great cathedrals of Britain; indeed, compared with others such as Ely, Durham or York it is almost a cottage. The most immediately striking difference is that it is not built of hard grey stone, capable of fantastic and intricate development, but of the friable red sandstone of the locality. Belonging as it does to the early

medieval period (building was started in 1092), it is an altogether plainer construction. It neither overwhelms nor amazes. There was a church on this site in Anglo-Saxon times. Hugh Lupus, the first of the Norman earls of Chester, founded a Benedictine abbey here, and it flourished until the Dissolution of the Monasteries in the reign of Henry VIII. Although the monastic foundation was suppressed in 1540, the building itself escaped devastation because in the following year it was made the cathedral of the newly formed diocese of Chester.

Nearest the walls is the lady chapel (**50**), built in 1260–80 but heavily restored in the 19th century, with a great east window of five straight lancets, with glass designed in 1859 by William Wailes. To the right of this, across the green, are the original monastic buildings. The chapter house also has five lancets, which tend towards each other like praying hands; the well-proportioned tracery dates from about 1250. To the right again, the more elaborate window of the refectory is a 19th-century restoration by Sir George Gilbert Scott (1811–78), one of several important architects responsible for an immense amount of rebuilding and elaboration throughout the entire building. He added the high pointed tower to the left of the lady chapel, seen across the Cheshire Regiment Memorial Garden. In the south-east corner of the garden, close to the walls, is the new belfry, the Addleshaw Tower (1974), named after Dean Addleshaw (1906–82), a devoted historian of the cathedral. It is the first detached bell tower built for any English cathedral since the 15th century and was needed because the bell frame in the central tower of the cathedral was badly decayed – renewing the frame would have put the tower itself at risk. A complex piece of engineering in a deceptively simple structure, it houses thirteen bells – a ring of twelve and a flat sixth. Following an old tradition, each bell is named after a saint venerated in Chester. One is named after St Edith (962–84), the daughter of King Edgar (see p. 14). Steps lead down to the south porch, the main visitors' entrance. Just inside the Memorial Garden gateway at the top of St Werburgh Street, at the south end of the south transept, look up at the amusing corbels (the small decorative blocks supporting the ledge) which, among several fantasies, have recognisable likenesses of two Victorian prime ministers, Gladstone and Disraeli.

The south porch leads into the immense south transept, which dates from the early 14th century. The ground plan of the cathedral (see p. 66) is cruciform. Its arms are, unusually, asymmetric, this side being much more spacious than the cramped north transept, which the monks could not have enlarged without pulling down part of their living quarters.

With the exception of the four early-20th-century chapels opposite the south porch and of the great west window, all the cathedral stained glass belongs to the 19th century; the windows in the south transept are pleasantly restrained in colour. To the left of these more modern chapels is the south choir aisle, the Chapel of St Erasmus, kept as a quiet place for prayer, undisturbed by visitors. The wrought-iron gate is Spanish, one of a 16th-century pair given to the cathedral in 1871.

The cathedral is full of interesting memorials, both personal and public. On the wall to the left of the entrance is a little tablet, 'sacred to the memory of Anna aged three weeks, Emily Diana aged two years and a half, William Pierrepont aged four and a half. Children of John Uniacke Esqr., of Great Boughton in this parish, and Anna his wife.' It bears no date or explanation; the style suggests that this family tragedy happened early in the 19th century.

The Royal Air Force memorial on the west wall of the south transept must surely be the most modest and touching of any in the land. It has a beautiful laminated wood propellor, a folded banner in a glass case, and the quiet rubric: 'Here therefore pray of your charity for the Royal Air Force and all who venture dear lives in the air.'

Towards the central tower and a little to the left is a cabinet containing pictures and the Roll of Honour of *HMS Chester*, with the Admiral's citation for the boy Jack Cornwell VC, the hero of the Battle of Jutland (1916): he 'was mortally wounded early in the action. He nevertheless remained standing alone at a most exposed post till the end of the action, with the gun's crew dead and wounded all around him. He was sixteen and a half years.'

A plaque above the Cornwell memorial tells of Frederick Philips, born in New York in 1720; he opposed the rebellion in North America, and 'was Proscribed and his Estate, one of the largest in New York, was Confiscated by the Usurped Legislature of that Province'. He fled to England and died in Chester in 1785, and was buried here in the south transept.

**46** *The town hall (1869), the dominant feature of Northgate Street, reproduces a European-medieval style much favoured by its Belfast architect, W. H. Lynn, who was also responsible for the parliament buildings in Sydney, Australia. It contains mayoral offices, Council Chamber and committee rooms, and magistrates' courts. Some civic records and insignia are kept here (others are in the Grosvenor Museum), and also the city's collection of silver plate. This includes a 14-inch silver oar, which was made in 1719 to be carried before the mayor on ceremonial occasions, and recalls his title of Admiral of the Dee, held when the city was the foremost port of the north-west – a memory that is occasionally revived when the mayor carries out official duties in connection with the river.*

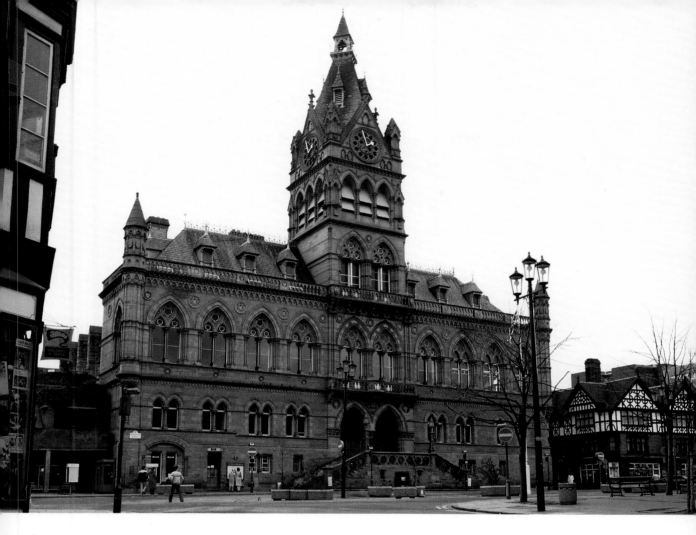

Crossing the nave in front of the choir, we come to the north transept. This is the oldest part of the cathedral, with characteristically rounded Norman arches and slightly pointed Early English ones. It has a splendid timbered ceiling dating from about 1520, maintained in beautiful condition. The small space is dominated by a vast tomb of imaginative Victorian design, made for Bishop Pearson, who died in 1686. He was important as the author of an *Exposition of the Creed*, a work which was influential in the subsequent drawing up of the familiar form of *The Book of Common Prayer* (1662), the prayer book used in Anglican churches throughout the last three centuries. High on the wall is a monument by the fashionable 18th-century sculptor Nollekens; it shows a child weeping over an urn, but it is placed rather too high for detailed appreciation. The great curiosity here, however, is the cobweb picture of a madonna and child, thought to have been painted by a Tyrolean artist in the late 18th century, copied from a painting by Cranach (1472–1553); apparently painting on cobwebs was an art which flourished in the Tyrol from 1750 onwards. It is softly lit from behind, and has a delicacy and charm not usually associated with Cranach. No one knows how it came to be here.

We now go through the second of the Spanish wrought-iron gates and along the north choir aisle, past the colourful stained-glass Nativity at the east end (1857, by A. and M. O'Connor), pausing to note the fine marble roundel

portrait of Bishop Jacobson (died 1884) by Queen Victoria's favourite sculptor, Boehm, after a design by Sir A. W. Blomfield.

Turning right at the end of the north choir aisle, we enter the well-lit lady chapel, built before the present choir in the latter part of the 13th century and restored to its original form by Sir George Gilbert Scott in 1868–73. The east window (seen earlier from the walls) shows scenes from the life of Christ; the north window has medallions depicting the ministry of St Peter; and the three south windows describe the life of St Paul, also in medallions. The three great bosses in the 13th-century roof vaulting show the murder of St Thomas à Becket at Canterbury in 1170, the Virgin and Child, and the Trinity.

At the west end of the lady chapel is the early-14th-century shrine of St Werburgh, ravaged by time, and restored in part by Sir A. W. Blomfield with some fragments found in the baptistery and plain sandstone blocks. Until 1876 the shrine was used as the base of the Bishop's throne. Both the Anglo-Saxon church and the abbey on this site were dedicated to St Werburgh (who is now also commemorated in the name of a modern street in the city and in

**47, 48** *Two of Chester's many ancient inns, both in Northgate Street. Above, the 16th-century Pied Bull still displays a board announcing distant destinations reached by coach from here in the time of stage coaches. The frontage over the pavement was added in the 18th century. Right, The Blue Bell, dating from the 15th century, is thought to be Chester's oldest domestic building.*

62

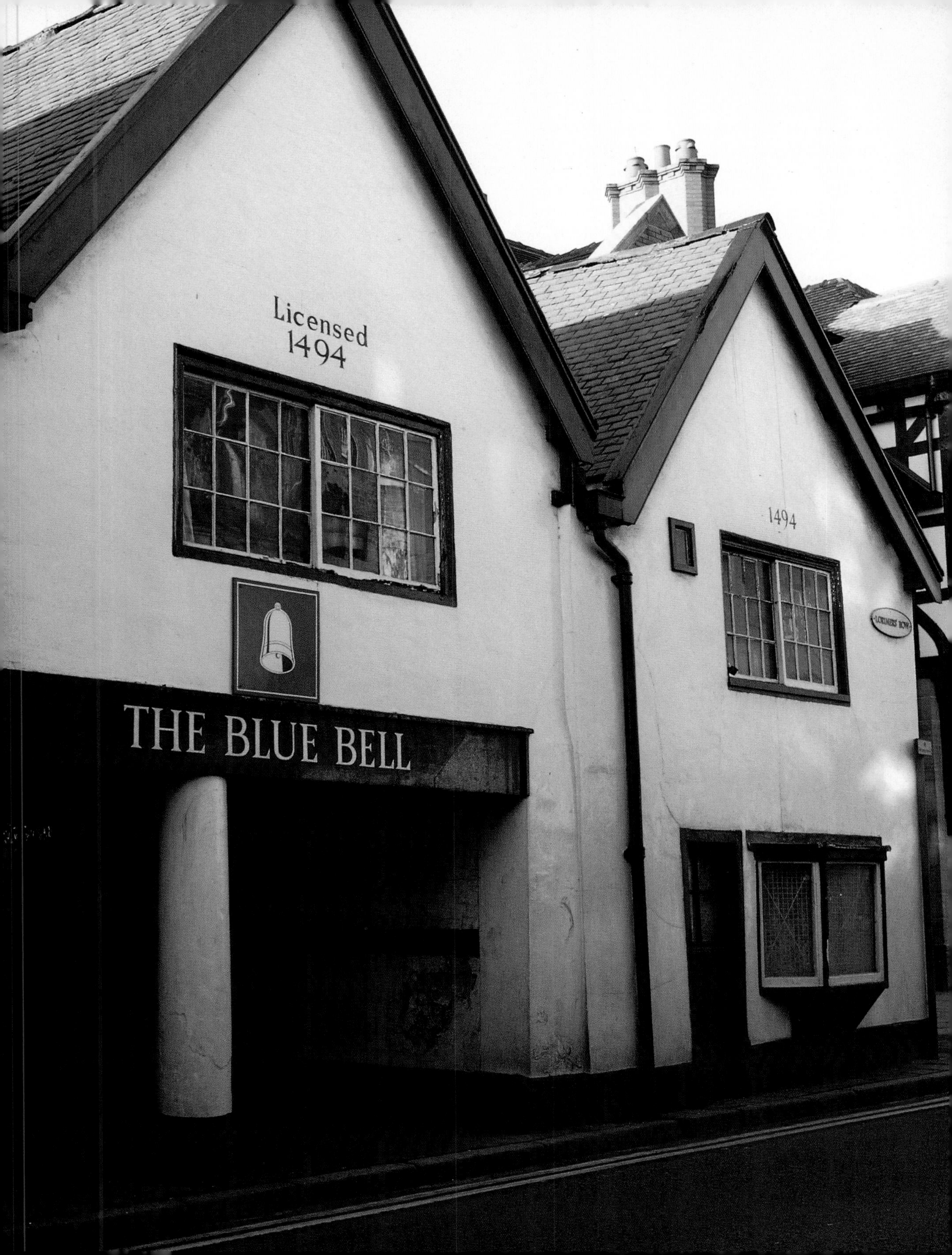
Licensed
1494
THE BLUE BELL
1494

the dedication of the Roman Catholic church in Grosvenor Park Road). She was an Anglo-Saxon princess and abbess, daughter of Wulfhere, king of Mercia (the present-day Midlands), and lived in the later years of the 7th century; a woman of formidable piety and powerful connections, with several sainted aunts and a revered grandmother, St Sexburg, all of whom are depicted in the modern window in the cathedral refectory. She first became a nun at Ely, lived most of her life at Weedon, Northamptonshire, died at Threckingham, Lincolnshire, and was buried at Hanbury, a monastery in Staffordshire. A few years later her body was found to be miraculously uncorrupted, and her shrine became an object of veneration. It was moved for safety to the church in Chester in the early years of the 10th century when the Danes were overrunning the country; the shrine we see here was made about the year 1310.

**49** *The front of Retreat House, Abbey Square, part of the cathedral precinct off Northgate Street. The harmonious similarity of these Georgian houses is enhanced by the variety of original detail both inside and out.*

**50** *The east end of the cathedral, with the Georgian houses of Abbey Street in the distance. In the centre, behind the trees, is the 13th-century lady chapel. The steep pitched polygonal roof to the left, at the end of the south choir aisle, is a fanciful addition by Sir George Gilbert Scott, who also restored the pinnacles of the 14th-century tower.*

A small happy light is cast on the so-called Dark Ages in a story told about St Werburgh in an account of her life written by a Flemish monk, Goscelin, who was working in Canterbury at the end of the 10th century. A flock of wild geese had descended on the estate at Weedon, causing great damage, so St Werburgh told a farm-hand to command them to let themselves be rounded up and penned in. He did so, not without some sturdy misgivings, and to his astonishment, says Goscelin, 'not one bird from all that gathering raised a wing, but like wingless chicks, or as if they had had their wings cut off, they moved on foot, walking with bowed heads as if ashamed of their bad behaviour. So they assembled within the courtyard of their judge, trembling and subdued as if found guilty.' The next morning St Werburgh ordered that they should be pardoned and set free, and they flew off, only to discover that one of their number was missing – it had been stolen during the night and hidden by one of the farm servants. They 'gathered above the virgin's house and bewailed with a great din the harm done to their fellow creature . . . So at the noise and complaint of the great host, the divine virgin went out and understood its cause . . . Straightway the theft was investigated and the culprit himself admitted it. The holy peacemaker took the bird back and reunited it with its tribe, and ordered it to be off immediately on the conditions previously given.' (Translated from the Latin by N. J. Munday, 1973.)

The theft of the goose is portrayed in a carving on one of the misericords in the choir, to which we come next. The choir contains a wealth of superb wood

65

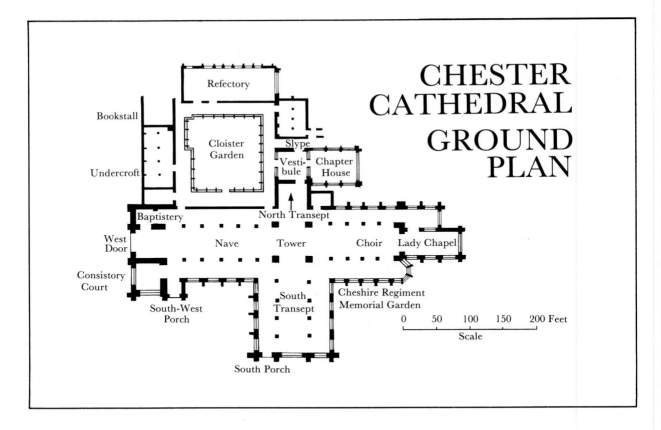

**CHESTER CATHEDRAL GROUND PLAN**

Refectory

Bookstall

Cloister Garden

Slype

Undercroft

Vesti-bule

Chapter House

Baptistery

North Transept

West Door

Nave

Tower

Choir

Lady Chapel

Consistory Court

South Transept

Cheshire Regiment Memorial Garden

South-West Porch

0    50    100    150    200 Feet

Scale

South Porch

carving (**52, 53**) which is the greatest treasure of the cathedral, having survived for more than 600 years with remarkably little sign of wear or damage. The entire stalls have undergone several moves, and a certain amount of recarving and alteration was done in the 1860s and 70s. Unfortunately, five misericords were destroyed in the 19th century by Dean Howson, on the grounds that they 'were very improper'. The only other places in England with anything comparable are Lincoln cathedral, Nantwich church in Cheshire (see p. 87), and Manchester cathedral, which is later. The exquisite finesse of the pinnacled canopies over the stalls make an astonishing contrast with the frequently earthy, even rugged, subject matter of many of the bench and misericord carvings below: men wrestle, couples quarrel, foxes steal grapes, angels play lutes, biblical scenes are flanked by monsters and mythological figures from distant pre-Christian cultures – all of the utmost liveliness and fascination. 'The restored goose' from the story of St Werburgh recounted above (with the culprit detected on the left and confessing on the right) is on the sixth misericord on the north side, at the end of the choir nearest the screen. (Misericords, the small carved ledges on the undersides of the tip-up seats of the choir stalls, take their name from the Latin word for pity – they were intended to be leant upon for rest during interminable hours of standing through services.) The fine choir screen (**51**) was designed by Sir Giles Gilbert Scott in the 1870s, and is in keeping with the earlier carved work.

We now enter the nave, the main body of the church; the south side was

**51** *The elaborately carved choir screen (1876) and wrought-iron gates at the central crossing of the cathedral were designed by Sir George Gilbert Scott, who was responsible for a large part of the restoration work here; the choir stalls were originally further down the nave, and he moved them to their present position.*

started about 1360, the north side about a hundred years later. The great west window has vigorous stained glass by W. T. Carter-Shapland (1961), depicting Our Lady and the English saints, and is particularly attractive when the late afternoon sun shines through it. To its left, on the ground floor of the uncompleted south-west tower and entered through a screen, is the only surviving example in England of a furnished 17th-century consistory court, an ecclesiastical court presided over by the bishop's judge, the chancellor of the diocese, and still used for various kinds of church legal transactions. The furnishings and the screen date from 1636, when the court was established here, in the time of Bishop Bridgeman. His arms, as well as those of Hugh Lupus, appear on the canopy over the chancellor's throne. To the right of the west window, in the north-west corner, is the oldest part of the nave, its original Norman end, with imposing rounded arches, built about 1140; this corner is now the baptistery, and the font, from Venice, is 19th century. On the north wall there are some melancholy greenish mosaics of scenes from the lives of Abraham, Moses, David and Elijah, designed by the stained-glass artist J. R. Clayton in the 1880s, and to the right of them a door takes us from the cathedral into the monastic buildings.

The cloisters surround a small garden and fountain, the site of the monks' reservoir. In the Middle Ages they were the centre of the life of the monastery and the recesses between the columns were used as carrels, i.e. private study areas, in which the monks sat to copy manuscripts. They have undergone several periods of rebuilding, particularly in the early 16th century and shortly

**52** *Example of the cathedral's rich wood carvings, one of the misericords. These carvings, under the seats of the choir stalls, range from the naturalism of domestic scenes, such as a couple quarrelling or a wrestling match, through myth and legend (Tristan and Isolde) and symbolism (a figure rising from a shell, fighting dragons), to religious scenes (St Werburgh and the goose).*

before the first world war, but there is still some Norman work on the south side. The glass in the arcade windows, which illustrate the calendar of the Church of England, was added in the 1920s. A few steps along the east side is the vestibule, an ante-room with stone seats ranged around the walls, and remarkable for the simple columns which spring into the vaulted roof without interruption or ornament. The vestibule leads into the rib-vaulted chapter house, the aesthetic climax of the cathedral. This finely proportioned room is still the administrative centre, as it has been since monastic times, and contains part of the cathedral library. The lancet windows have good indigo, brown and white glass made in 1872.

The slype is an ancient passage which led to the infirmary and across the green to the Kaleyard Gate. The monks used this gate in the walls to reach their kitchen gardens (kale-yards).

In the north cloister we pass the *lavatorium*, the monks' wash place, and come to the door of the refectory, where the archway all too clearly illustrates the friable quality of Cheshire sandstone. The refectory, though basically Norman, belongs to the 13th and 14th centuries; the windows were altered in the 15th century, giving it the appearance of a later building. In the wall on the right as we face the east window is a beautiful pulpit where a monk would read to his brothers as they ate; the stair to the pulpit is within the thickness of the wall, lit by five small, closely set windows, only visible from the cloister garden. The superb hammer-beam roof is a modern reconstruction (1939) by

*53 St Werburgh Row, opposite the south-west porch of the cathedral, looking towards Northgate Street. This is not a true Cestrian Row, in the form of a first floor gallery, but a modern arcade built in 1935 by Maxwell Ayrton. In the distance is the former King's School (now Barclays Bank), designed by Sir A. W. Blomfield in 1876.*

the architectural historian F. H. Crossley. Facing the window is a tapestry showing St Paul confronting the sorcerer Elymas, and up till 1843 it hung across the east end of the choir behind the high altar. It is one of several scenes from the Acts of the Apostles, woven at the Mortlake tapestry works in the time of Charles I and based on Raphael's cartoons for tapestries for the Sistine Chapel. Today the refectory is used for a variety of activities – meetings, concerts, wedding parties – and is a valued centre of social life for both cathedral and city.

The next entrance on the north cloister brings us to the pleasant modern bookshop, situated in relative obscurity (a welcome contrast to the blatant commercialism of certain more famous cathedrals). The north and west cloisters are very much the working end of the whole cathedral complex, with workshops in the Norman undercroft, and practice rooms for choristers.

Leaving the cathedral by the south-west porch near the end of the nave, we come out into St Werburgh Street. The arcade, St Werburgh Row (**53**), is a surprisingly modern addition, built in 1935, and it harmonises successfully with the original Rows of Eastgate Street, Bridge Street and Watergate Street. To our left, opposite the end of the Row, is Godstall Lane, once known as Music Hall Passage. The building at its north end was a theatre, graced by such stars as Sarah Siddons, in 1786, and Edmund Kean, in 1815; Charles Dickens, too, gave some of his famous readings here. Its fortunes declined, from Theatre Royal to Music Hall to cinema to supermarket, and it is now a clothes shop. A few steps bring us to Eastgate Street and Northgate Street.

## Walk 4: Bridge Street, Lower Bridge Street, the Castle and the Riverside

A walk from the Cross down the east side of Bridge Street gives us the opportunity to view the variety of architectural styles on the opposite side, and to visit three particular buildings. At street level, No. 39 has a well-preserved hypocaust (see p. 54) and Roman bath. No. 49, on the Row, a genuine survivor from the 17th century, was once St Michael's Rectory. It has carefully restored galleries, and some wood carving which includes six of an incomplete series of Stations of the Cross (**54**); these are plaster casts of the 17th-century originals, which were sold to an American buyer by the former owner, an antique dealer.

At the corner by the crossroads is St Michael's church, now the Heritage Centre, the first of its kind; it was opened in 1975 to commemorate European Architectural Heritage Year. Standing on part of the site of the south gateway of the Roman fortress, it houses a comprehensive display of all aspects of Chester's architecture, explaining the use of local materials and providing fascinating information about conservation, listed buildings, and the finances of restoration. An audio-visual theatre presents twenty-minute shows of over 300 slides with a taped commentary – a vivid picture of Chester, past and present. The oldest remaining parts of St Michael's are the north arcade and the beautifully carved and decorated chancel roof, which is said to date from 1496. Like the Guildhall (see Walk 1) the Heritage Centre demonstrates the practical and imaginative use of a deconsecrated church.

**54** *Inside St Michael's Rectory, Bridge Street. Six carved panels remain of a 17th-century series of nine Stations of the Cross in this rambling building (now a dress shop), which won an award for conservation in 1975.*

**55** *Outstanding wall paintings in the Chapel of St Mary de Castro, on the first floor of the Agricola Tower, which were brought to light by a conservation programme undertaken by English Heritage and the Courtauld Institute of Art in May 1992. Reminiscent of manuscript illumination in their small scale and exquisite quality, they form the most significant survival of medieval wall painting in north-west England. Seen here, the Visitation on the vault of the chapel.*
*The paintings date from the first half of the 13th century, and were probably executed either for the powerful Earl Ranulf III of Chester (d.1232) or for Henry III who took over the castle in 1237 after the death of the last earl.*

**56** *The Agricola Tower, the only remaining part of the grim medieval castle, seen here from the south-west. The whole tower has been much restored and was completely re-faced in the 19th century.*

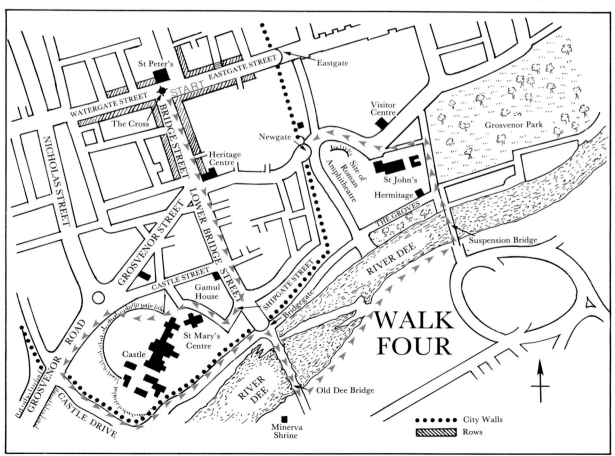

We continue over the crossroads. The Falcon, on the corner diagonally opposite St Michael's, was once the town house of the Grosvenor family (see p. 25), and dates from the 17th century. It was considerably altered at the end of the last century, and again more recently; a Row went through its first floor at one time, though no trace of this now remains. Opposite, the very pretty Tudor Houses date from 1503. A little further down on the same (west) side, Gamul House has an exterior gallery – the remains of a Row – and some unusual elliptical windows. This is the house where Charles I is supposed to have stayed during the siege of Chester (see p. 19). Two exceptionally handsome 17th-century houses near the Bridgegate, best seen from the walls (see Walk 2), are both inns, The Old King's Head and The Bear and Billet (**40**).

The sector within the angle of Lower Bridge Street and Shipgate Street is one of interesting renewal, completed 1988–9. Heritage Court (**21**), reached through a low, cambered archway on the right, is worth the few steps of detour: a 17th-century streetfront has been restored over the archway, and within is an attractive bricked court, where the buildings, intended for offices, are alternately white plaster and brick. Lower down the street, the new Shipgate House development provides a variety of domestic housing designed by James Sanders – flats and houses grouped round a paved courtyard and overlooking the river.

Now we turn right into Shipgate Street and climb St Mary's Hill, an exceptionally steep and cobbled road which was once the pack-horse route

**57, 58** *The pleasant tree-lined promenade known as the Groves extends along the river from the Old Dee Bridge as far as the suspension bridge. Through much of the year, and especially in summer, this is a great centre of leisure activity, including rowing, canoeing, fishing and strolling; and regattas and canoeing competitions are held along this stretch of the river. Below, the 19th-century bandstand.*

from the city centre to the river. It brings us to another deconsecrated church, St Mary's-on-the-Hill, now a study centre. The church has been carefully restored and has a beautiful Tudor roof with gilded bosses. It is used for meetings, exhibitions, and by Cheshire schools studying the city of Chester. In one account of a visit to the centre, a seven-year-old from a local school wrote: 'When we got there we went to St Mary's center and watched a film about yousing your eyes and ears. Then we went down the river for lunch.'

The top of St Mary's Hill leads to the castle, where the nearest wing is occupied by the Cheshire Regiment Museum. The collection consists mainly of hand weapons, medals and uniforms, and will appeal to the visitor with an interest in military history.

Pevsner considers Thomas Harrison's rebuilding of Chester castle (begun in 1788 but not completed until 1822) 'one of the most powerful monuments of the Greek Revival in the whole of England'. The central block has an impressive portico of Doric columns. Immediately inside is the chamber of the Crown Court (courts of justice), semi-circular, with a beautiful coffered roof and skylight reminiscent of the Pantheon in Rome. The western wing is the regimental officers' mess. What remains of the ancient castle lies behind this, not visible from the main courtyard. It is the Agricola Tower (**55, 56**), to be seen from outside as we continue along the walls towards the Old Dee Bridge (see Walk 2). Leaving the castle by the front archway and turning left, we could make a quiet and contrasting diversion by continuing over the Grosvenor Bridge to the pleasantly gloomy Victorian cemetery on the other side of the river, and then return to retrace a section of the walk on the walls, along Castle Drive to the Old Dee Bridge (back cover).

Across the river, in a sombre little park beside the Ship Inn, known as Edgar's Field, is a Roman shrine, said to be dedicated to the goddess Minerva. It does not contain anything resembling a goddess but there is a faint suggestion of carving in the rocky outcrop, which is what remains of a Roman quarry. From here we have by far the best view of the bridge, as the white waters of the weir are highlighted between the dark arches.

We keep to the south side of the river, and recross it by the suspension bridge (**39**), built in 1852. This brings us to the Groves (**57** and **58**) and Grosvenor Park. A few yards to the left as we leave the bridge, and across a green, is a little house associated with the unfortunate King Harold (see p. 13). The reticulated tracery of the first-floor window facing the green gives the house a gothic appearance; it is known variously as the Hermitage or the Anchorite's Cell.

A path up through the park leads to St John's church. This is a fine Norman building with strong columns and rounded arches, all in a light, pinkish stone, which looks fresher and healthier than the sandstone of the cathedral. It is built on the site of a church founded in the late 6th or early 7th century. There are three medieval stone effigies, and 17th-century painted memorials by members of the prominent Randle Holme family, of whom several were mayors of Chester and one was a diligent archivist. In the north aisle is a medieval wall painting of St John the Baptist (**59**). Outside, the ruins (**6**) speak of greater size and importance in former times: this was the collegiate and cathedral church of Chester in the 11th century. After the see was transferred to Coventry in 1102 it remained a collegiate church until the Dissolution. It then became a parish church and parts of the building fell out of use, so that the east end of the chancel, the lady chapel and the choir chapels built in the 14th century are now only ruins. All that remains as a place of worship is most of the nave, with the north and south aisles, the crossing and the west end of the chancel. The Victorian appearance of the exterior is partly a result of the restoration work by R. C. Hussey in the 1860s. It suffered a calamity in 1881 when the west tower collapsed. Enough money was raised to rebuild a reproduction (by John Douglas) of the Early English porch but not to reconstruct the tower.

Over the road is the Visitor Centre, a useful and cheerful place which provides souvenirs, refreshments, information, accommodation bookings, and brass rubbing. Opposite is the amphitheatre (see p. 11), and across again a high section of Roman and medieval wall. From here we can return to the city centre, either by Newgate bridge and the walls to Eastgate Street, or along Pepper Street and Bridge Street.

**59** *A medieval wall painting of St John the Baptist on one of the massive columns in the nave of St John's church. No painting has survived on any of the other columns. The church had cathedral status, in the diocese of Lichfield and Coventry, until about 1540, when the new diocese of Chester was established. Building began in 1075, on an earlier Saxon site, and continued into the 13th century. It is an especially grand and powerful piece of Norman architecture (Early English in the later, upper parts); the great columns lean very slightly outwards – the only known instance of this technique in England.*

# The Zoo

Chester Zoo owes its existence to the energy and passion of one man, George Mottershead (1894–1978), whose remarkable gift with animals was united with a single-minded vision and tenacity. As a boy he had been horrified to see elephants shackled in zoos, and he conceived an ambition to show animals in the most natural surroundings compatible with safety – an idea which is taken for granted nowadays, but which then was near to revolutionary.

Modest beginnings were made on the present site in 1931, with George Mottershead putting up many of the buildings himself. In 1934, when support for the zoo was increasing, it became the North of England Zoological Society – a name it retained when it was recognised as an educational and charitable institution in 1950. Growth was steady in the pre-war years, and not altogether halted by the second world war, when animals evacuated from other zoos had to be accommodated; wartime shortages made it necessary to appeal to local people and firms for help in providing food, and in this way public support, which had previously been somewhat wavering, was extended and strengthened. Since 1950 the zoo has gone from strength to strength, holding an important place in the international zoological scene, breeding and exchanging animals in danger of extinction.

It is the largest and most beautiful zoo in the north of England and also among Britain's top tourist attractions. In 1983 there were over 800,000 visitors and there have been as many as a million in one year. Yet there is rarely any sense of overcrowding in its 110 acres. The gardens, tended by more than twenty gardeners, are informal, formal (15,000 roses) and specialised (e.g. South American). They are deservedly famous and represent a remarkable achievement, since they were not started until 1953.

The animal houses are enjoyable not only because of their inhabitants but also on account of the profusion of exotic plants flourishing in them: the elephant house has white jasmine (which occasioned the much-quoted remark of one visitor, 'I never knew elephants smelt like that!'); in the monkey house is a fine screen of bougainvillea, and a datura tree; the bird house entrance corridor is hung with baskets of exquisite fuchsias. Gorillas, alligators and smaller reptiles live in the tropical house, along with a wide variety of birds, many of which fly free – visitors on the upper walkway may find themselves quite close to humming-birds feeding from little nectar dispensers. Even in winter the entrance is ablaze with colour: cyclamen, orchids, and the thin red trumpets of columnia banksii. A forty-foot waterfall drops into a pool of giant carp, arched over with bromeliads, and the centre of the house is filled with banana trees.

Although winter is the season for stocktaking and cleaning, it is neverthe-

**60** *Sealions at Chester Zoo. From modest beginnings after the first world war the zoo has become one of Britain's major tourist attractions.*

less a good time for a visit. Few sights can be more consoling on a grey day in early February than the flamingoes standing brilliant scarlet and pink against a background of pale brown water and orange willow twigs; or, by contrast, the penguins seen through the glass sides of their new pool, swooping and diving and quarrelling at feeding time.

If a zoo is to be desired at all – a question which should perhaps be asked – then Chester Zoo must be one of the most desirable in the whole country.

**61** *Chimpanzees at Chester Zoo.*

# Places of Interest around Chester

*The following places are marked on the map at the end of the book.*

### Beeston Castle

About 15 miles south-east of Chester, on the B5152, is Beeston castle (**62**). This is the ruin of a fortress built around 1220 by Randle de Blundeville, 6th earl of Chester, on the site of a prehistoric hill fort. It is set on an isolated and dramatic rock standing 740 feet high; from this vantage point there are magnificent views across a great stretch of the county, including the semi-circle of hills and rocky outcrops that extends from Helsby and Delamere to the romantic 19th-century castle of nearby Peckforton (**74**). If the astronomers at Jodrell Bank (see p. 83) happen to be studying the heavens in a westerly direction, the huge white saucer of the telescope should be visible, 20 miles or so to the east.

### Ellesmere Port Boat Museum

Housed in a restored 19th-century dock complex, 8 miles north of Chester, between the Shropshire Union Canal and the Manchester Ship Canal, this unusual museum (**63**) boasts the largest collection of canal boats in Europe, ranging from a 19th-century mine boat to a 300-ton coaster. Other exhibits give a lively account of all the development of the canal system in this country, along with the steam engines which powered the hydraulic pumping station. It is possible to board some of the craft and see the intimate and uniquely decorated interiors of barge cabins.

### Hawarden Castle

Hawarden Castle (**9**) in North Wales, 7 miles west of Chester, stands on a hill which forms a natural defence, jutting out between the marshes of the Dee Estuary and the long line of the Clwyddian Hills. This spot marked the northern gateway to Wales. The castle has Saxon earthworks and the ruins of a 13th-century fortress, now romantically embowered in woodland. It is likely that the stone castle was built in the aftermath of Edward I's invasion of Wales in 1277. It was a strong outpost of royalist Chester during the Civil War. The house, built in 1752, was the home of the great Liberal prime minister, William Gladstone. He founded in Hawarden the St Deiniol Library, which is considered to be one of the best theological libraries in the country – it is residential, and open to anyone for private study, besides being a little theological college for six students.

## Holywell

This is the British Lourdes: St Winefride's Well (**64**) in North Wales, 20 miles north-west of Chester, has been a place of pilgrimage for over a thousand years, and probably the remarkably clear water was valued for its healing properties even in pagan times. Legend tells how the virgin Winefride was pursued by Caradoc, a horrible chieftain from Hawarden, who cut off her head when he could not have his way with her. She was restored to life by her uncle, St Bueno, who rejoined her head to her body, with only a white line round her neck to show what had happened. The well gushed forth from the place where her head had fallen.

The present chapel above the well, built at the end of the 15th century under the supervision of the abbot of nearby Basingwerk Abbey, received many fervent pilgrims prior to the Reformation. Ownership was contested when Henry VIII dissolved Basingwerk Abbey and it was the subject of a long-drawn-out struggle between Protestant and Catholic interests in recusant times (the reign of Elizabeth I), when Catholics were under extreme duress and persecution. In 1579 the Queen instructed the Council of Marches 'To discover all Papist activities and recommend measures for suppressing them . . . to pay particular attention to the pilgrimages to St Winefrede's Well.' The pilgrims nevertheless continued to make their way to Holywell. The chapel is a unique and lovely jewel of the 15th century, when the Lady Margaret Beaufort (mother of Henry VII) was its most celebrated patron.

From Holywell the Greenfield Valley Heritage Park goes for a mile and a half through woodland and lakeside to Basingwerk Abbey beside the River Dee. It is an area of interest for industrial archaeology because lead, mined here since Roman times, was processed in Chester from the late 18th century.

**62** *The gateway to the keep of Beeston castle, from the south. There is a dry moat in front and, on the other side, a dramatic rock face which drops more than 700 feet to the Cheshire Plain. It would appear to be unassailable, but in fact the castle has been in ruins for many centuries. Besides these 13th-century gatehouse towers there remain fragmentary curtain walls and towers on the east and south sides.*

82

## Jodrell Bank

Jodrell Bank (**65**), 30 miles east of Chester, is the University of Manchester's radio telescope. The huge white bowl which dominates the countryside around the little town of Holmes Chapel is the Mark I dish, the largest and oldest of five. Built in 1952–7, it is 250 feet in diameter, and is one of the largest fully steerable radio telescopes in the world. Jodrell Bank is the centre of a unique system of small telescopes known as MERLIN (Multi-Element Radio Linked Interferometer), with dishes spread across a hundred-mile sector of Wales and the west of England. Visitors are welcome and there is an information centre and a planetarium.

## Knutsford

Knutsford, 25 miles north-east of Chester, was the home of Elizabeth Gaskell, and the setting for her novel *Cranford* (1853); its narrow thoroughfares, and especially King Street, winding through the centre of the town, retain the charm and atmosphere of that period, and there is a good amount of Georgian building, including some pretty brick cottages at the south end of King Street and the Royal George Hotel further north. Mrs Gaskell recorded a custom which was remembered in her day, and thought to be peculiar to Knutsford: when there was a wedding the streets were covered with dark sand, overlaid

*63 The Boat Museum, Ellesmere Port, makes use of some of the old warehouses which were built around 1800 at the end of the Chester Canal, where it joins the River Mersey. This lively museum is the largest of its kind in Europe: boats, pumping engines, and other equipment effectively re-create the great days of canal traffic.*

with flowers – perhaps an ancient vestige of a fertility rite, related to the well-dressing tradition which persists in Derbyshire to this day.

There are some very surprising and outlandish public buildings in King Street, most notably the Gaskell Memorial Tower and King's Coffee House (1907), both by a late-19th-century eccentric, R. H. Watt. The courtyard of King's Coffee House was added in 1908 and is constructed using the neo-classical pillars of a demolished church in Manchester. The bizarre style is hard to define, but the motifs may be Italian or Byzantine. Legh Road, a right turn off the Chelford road as you leave Knutsford, boasts what Pevsner describes as the 'maddest sequence of villas in all England', most of which are flamboyantly Italianate. They are execrated by purists, but nevertheless are strangely lovable – and they could not happen now.

The great country estate of Tatton Hall lies 3 miles north of Knustford (Tatton Park itself extends to the north end of King Street), and offers all the interest and recreation of stately home, gardens (including a Japanese garden and a maze), a farm, and a thousand acres of parkland with opportunities for walking, swimming, fishing and sailing.

## Little Moreton Hall

Little Morteton Hall (**67**), 35 miles east of Chester, lies south of Congleton. It

**64** *For over a thousand years the shrine of St Winefride at Holywell, North Wales, has been a place of pilgrimage, for the water is supposed to possess curative properties. The well, seen here, is partially protected by a delightful medieval canopy; in front of it is a larger basin open to the sky. The water is absolutely clear and very cold. Originally there were slender pillars between each of the piers supporting the ceiling, and a stone screen divided the well itself from the part kept as a bathing place for the pilgrims.*

**65** *The great main dish of Jodrell Bank radio telescope was constructed in the mid 1950s, and completed in time to track the first sputnik. It is one of five dishes and dominates the flat countryside around Holmes Chapel, about 30 miles east of Chester.*

must certainly be the most famous and picturesque example of medieval half-timbered building in England, extravagantly elaborate, with a wealth of carving dating from the 16th century. The oldest part, the east wing and most of the Great Hall, was built by Sir Richard de Moreton in the 1440s and 50s and added to by successive generations of the Moreton family, as the fancy took them: the west wing and porch were added in 1480 and the east wing extension in the early 16th century; in the middle of the 16th century the bay windows were built (their overhangs almost touch and are connected by a kind of bridge); the south wing, including the famous long gallery on the uppermost floor, is less sturdy than the west wing and was added in 1570–80.

Apart from the brick chimneys and a few (later) buttresses, all is wood – a great tribute to the joiners' craft and superb understanding of their material. The gritstone slates came from Mow Cop (see p. 87) and the leaded windows are especially pretty. The house is surrounded by a moat and in the area of the garden to the north of the house is a knot garden. This was laid out in 1975 and based on a design in *The English Gardener*, which was published in 1688, although the design itself is probably Elizabethan in origin. Little Moreton Hall has been in the hands of the National Trust since 1938. Another comparable courtyard house of the same period, and well worth visiting, is Speke Hall, Liverpool.

## Marford

The village of Marford, a clutch of gingerbread houses situated 12 miles

south-west of Chester on either side of the narrow and busy road between Chester and Wrexham, evidently belongs to the Gothic revival of the late 18th century, when the vogue for the picturesque beguiled landlords into buildings of greater and greater fantasy. In this village they are on a humble scale, and it is all too easy to drive straight through the village and miss the many 'cottages ornés' (**66**), with irregular walls, projecting eaves and decorated gables, like so many which were charmingly commemorated in the china pastille burners of the same period. No one knows for certain who was responsible for Marford – it may have been one George Boscawen, of whom nothing is definitely known; it seems that landlords were mostly absent, and the village was preserved in the care of generations of devoted stewards. The houses are all now in private hands.

**66** One of the fanciful 'cottages ornés' to be seen in the village of Marford, south of Chester on the Wrexham road.

## Moel Fammau

Moel Fammau, 16 miles west of Chester, is the highest point of the Clwyddian Range, lying between Mold and Ruthin, well within the Welsh border, but very much part of the Chester scene. Indeed it has been nicknamed Cheshire's Mount Fuji, for wherever you go it is always there, as Fuji Yama is in Japanese prints. The ruin on the summit is all that remains of an unfinished tower which was intended to mark the jubilee of George III. Although not strictly a folly, it complements that of Mow Cop at the other end of the county (see below), and one can be seen from the other when the light is right. The views from the footpath to Moel Fammau are breathtaking.

**67** *Little Moreton Hall is the best known and most extraordinary black and white house in England. The moat forms an almost perfect square around the hall and only one bridge crosses it. Building began in the mid 15th century, and the south wing, pictured here, was added about 1570–80. It shows both square and ornamental panelling, styles of decorative timber framing found mainly in the West Midlands and the Welsh borders, as well as the local technique of coving – a concave plaster cove beneath an overhang or jetty.*

## Mow Cop

This sham ruin (**69**), consisting of a large round tower, a high and wide arch and some walling, was built in 1754, at a time when this was the fashionable way for landowners to improve and add interest to their views. It has a commanding position on a hilltop, which is over 1,000 feet high, south-east of Little Moreton Hall, about 36 miles east of Chester. The strange name simply means Hill with a Stack (from Old English *muga* meaning stack or heap, and *cop* meaning hill); there was a beacon recorded on this site in 1329. Its elevated position made it a suitable place for great revivalist gatherings in the earlier years of the last century, and the Primitive Methodist sect, a splinter group from the Wesleyan Methodists led by W. Clowes and H. Bourne, which flourished in the pottery towns of Staffordshire, originated here in 1805.

## Nantwich

Nantwich lies 20 miles south-east of Chester and is the most attractive of the three 'wiches' (salt towns); from Roman times until the mid 19th century it was a centre of the English salt industry. The church of St Mary is large and impressive: it was built in the 14th century and is particularly interesting

because the change in building style from Decorated to Perpendicular is abruptly evident. Compare, for example, the Decorated side windows of the chancel with the Perpendicular east window of seven lights. The finely carved canopies and misericords of the choir stalls, comparable with those in Chester cathedral, are late 14th century. Churche's Mansion (**68**), built by Thomas Cleese in 1577, is the only domestic building earlier than 1583, when there was a disastrous fire; the timber-framed Crown Hotel dates from soon after that. Joseph Priestley, chemist, philosopher, and discoverer of oxygen, was minister in the Unitarian Chapel here for a few years around 1758.

The A51 from Chester to Nantwich touches the edge of Delamere Forest, once the medieval hunting preserve of the earls of Chester, where belts of Scots pine and mixed woodland nowadays provide the setting for pleasant picnic areas. The rolling farmland in this area east of Chester formed part of the estates of the medieval Cistercian abbey of Vale Royal, founded by Edward I. A large house was built on the site in the 16th century and there is now virtually no trace of the abbey.

## Northwich Salt Museum

The Salt Museum in Northwich, 18 miles east of Chester, sheds light on the industrial history of the area. It explains the operation of salt working in Cheshire from Roman times to the present day, and gives a graphic account of the ways in which it has altered the landscape. The films should not be missed

*68 Churche's Mansion, Nantwich, a decorated half-timbered merchant's house built in 1577, lies on the outskirts of the town on the way to Crewe. It is now a restaurant. Some of the upper rooms have coloured plaster between the beams, said to be the original style of decoration, and something of a shock for eyes accustomed to white.*

**69** *Mow Cop Hill, south of Congleton, is over 1,000 feet high and is related geologically to the Peak District, which abuts on Cheshire further east. It is the oldest rock in the county. This so-called castle is a mid-18th-century folly, or sham ruin, built for Randle Wilbraham, who lived at nearby Rode Hall.*

— they tell a harrowing story of the devastation caused by subsidence in the last century, and show how the problems have been overcome by new methods developed by Imperial Chemical Industries. Unlike Nantwich, Northwich kept its industrial prosperity until it could switch over to chemicals.

The Anderton Boat Lift (**16**; see p. 24), is just north of here in the village of Anderton.

## Norton Priory, Runcorn

The Augustinian priory was founded 15 miles north-east of Chester in the 12th century and was elevated to the status of abbey in 1391. At the time of the Dissolution the buildings and lands, bought for £1,500, became the seat of the Brooke family. They built a Tudor mansion which was later replaced by a Georgian country house. This in turn was demolished, in 1928, and the site became an overgrown wilderness.

The Development Corporation of Runcorn New Town began work on the ruined priory in 1970. Their far-sighted plan, which at first supported much valuable archaeological study, has come to remarkable fruition, with an imaginative and prize-winning museum showing ancient building methods, aspects of monastic life, and sample remains, including rare fragments of tile-mosaic floors. The pattern of excavated church foundations can be seen from a viewing platform, and the Norman undercroft is restored (**70**). The beautiful Norman doorway is the finest to survive in Cheshire. Gardens have been lavishly planted, including a border of camellias near the entrance and a pergola of laburnum beyond the church stones. As they mature, they promise to become a most delightful retreat and to enhance the museum and excavations.

The 11-foot-high statue of St Christopher carrying Christ (**71**) was brought to Norton in the late 14th century. It stood in the grounds of the later houses and was moved to Liverpool Museum in 1964 before being returned to Norton when the excavations were complete.

The route from Chester to Runcorn passes the little towns of Frodsham and Helsby. Helsby Rock is a nursery for mountaineers, and although it is only

**70, 71** *Norton Priory, near Runcorn, the site of a great medieval monastery. The Norman undercroft* (below) *was restored in the 1970s. Right, the medieval statue of St Christopher in the undercroft. He was an appropriate second patron for the monastery, because the nearby Mersey was a dangerous river for travellers to cross.*

462 feet high, the views from its summit encompass Shropshire's Long Mynd, the nearer Welsh hills and even, on the clearest days, the Isle of Man. At night this same route through the industrial landscape of the River Mersey changes dramatically and takes on an astonishing brilliance.

## Port Sunlight

The first Lord Leverhulme founded Port Sunlight (on the Mersey Estuary, about 12 miles north-west of Chester) in 1888, to accommodate his soap-factory workers in optimum conditions of low density housing, with plenty of gardens and other amenities. He envisaged a village community in which people would be able to 'live and be comfortable' and 'learn that there is more enjoyment to life than in the mere going to and returning from work'. Building continued for about thirty years in a variety of attractively picturesque styles: traditional half-timbered black and white houses predominate, but there are obvious French, Flemish and German influences in the houses built up to 1905. Many of the homes were designed by local architects, including William Owen and John Douglas, and some (**72**) are by London architects such as Edwin Lutyens. The whole village has recently been designated a conservation area, as being a place of outstanding historic and architectural interest.

**72** *These workers' houses in Port Sunlight were built in 1897; they were designed by Edwin Lutyens and have his favourite Venetian-style windows. The generously planned model industrial village is full of attractive houses designed in many different styles by some of the best architects of the turn of the century. They have been modernised without altering their appearance and some are now privately owned: Like Chester, the village has its own Heritage Centre.*

**73** The Beguiling of Merlin *by Edward Burne-Jones is an example of the fine collection of Pre-Raphaelite works exhibited in the Lady Lever Gallery, Port Sunlight. This painting, one of a group of eight commissioned by Frederick Leyland and first shown at the Grosvenor Gallery Exhibition in 1877, depicts Merlin being lulled to sleep by the enchantress Nimüe, with whom he had fallen in love.*

Although it was not the first such manufacturer's village (Bromborough Pool Village, a mile south-east of Port Sunlight, was built in 1853 by Price's Patent Candle Company), it is unusual in that it has retained its original boundaries and it makes a fascinating oasis in the industrial landscape north of Chester.

The Lady Lever Gallery is surely the most exquisite small museum in England. It has been listed as one of the 200 most interesting art museums in the world. It contains treasures of Chinese porcelain and ceramics dating from 200 BC to the 18th century; furniture beautifully displayed in rooms of several distinct periods, one of which is a rare Napoleon room; Wedgwood china in great variety; English watercolours; and fashionable academic paintings of the 19th and 20th centuries (**73**). Artists represented include Ford Madox Brown, Burne-Jones, Constable, Gainsborough, Holman Hunt, Millais, Reynolds, Stubbs, Turner and De Wint. One painting in particular has a local interest, relating to the Gothic Eaton Hall (see p. 25): Turner's picture of Hafod in Cardiganshire (thought to be the original inspiration for Coleridge's poem 'Kubla Khan') shows a little palace of exactly the same style and period as the Eaton Hall represented more crudely in oils in the Grosvenor Museum. Such houses must have been a delight to behold, if not to live in.

**74** *The romantic silhouette of Peckforton castle in its superb setting south of Beeston, on a ridge of wooded hills which curve towards the River Dee at the Welsh border. This exact and 'learnedly executed' replica of a medieval castle was built during the 1840s by the distinguished architect Anthony Salvin, to the order of the first Lord Tollemache, who was enormously wealthy but earned the praise of Gladstone himself as a beneficent landlord.*

# PLACES OF INTEREST AROUND CHESTER

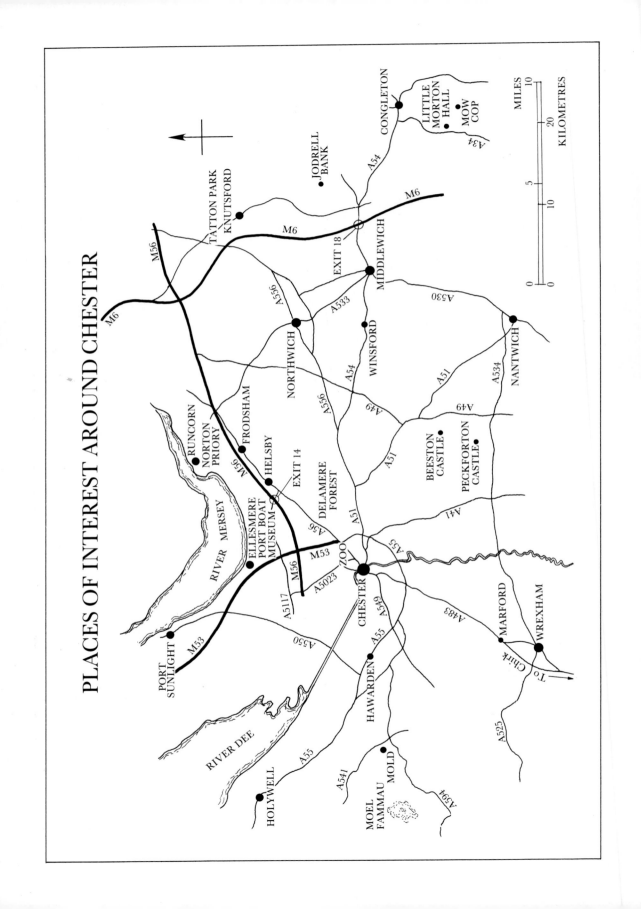